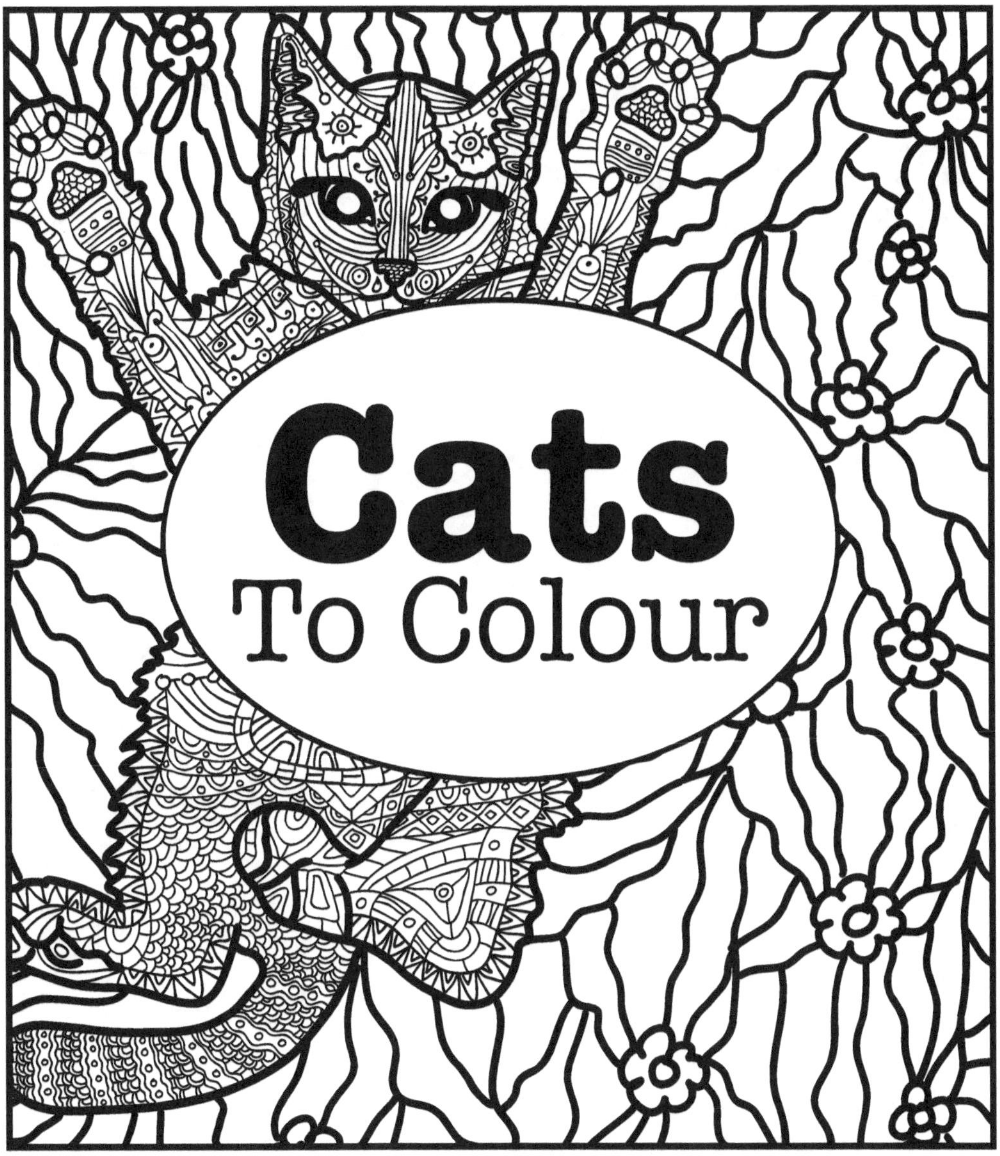

Cats
To Colour

Really **Relaxing** Colouring **Book 20**

First published in 2016 by Kyle Craig Publishing

Editor: Alison McNicol

Cover Design: Julie Anson

ISBN: 978-1-78595-228-9

A CIP record for this book is available from the British Library.

A Kyle Craig Publication

www.kyle-craig.com

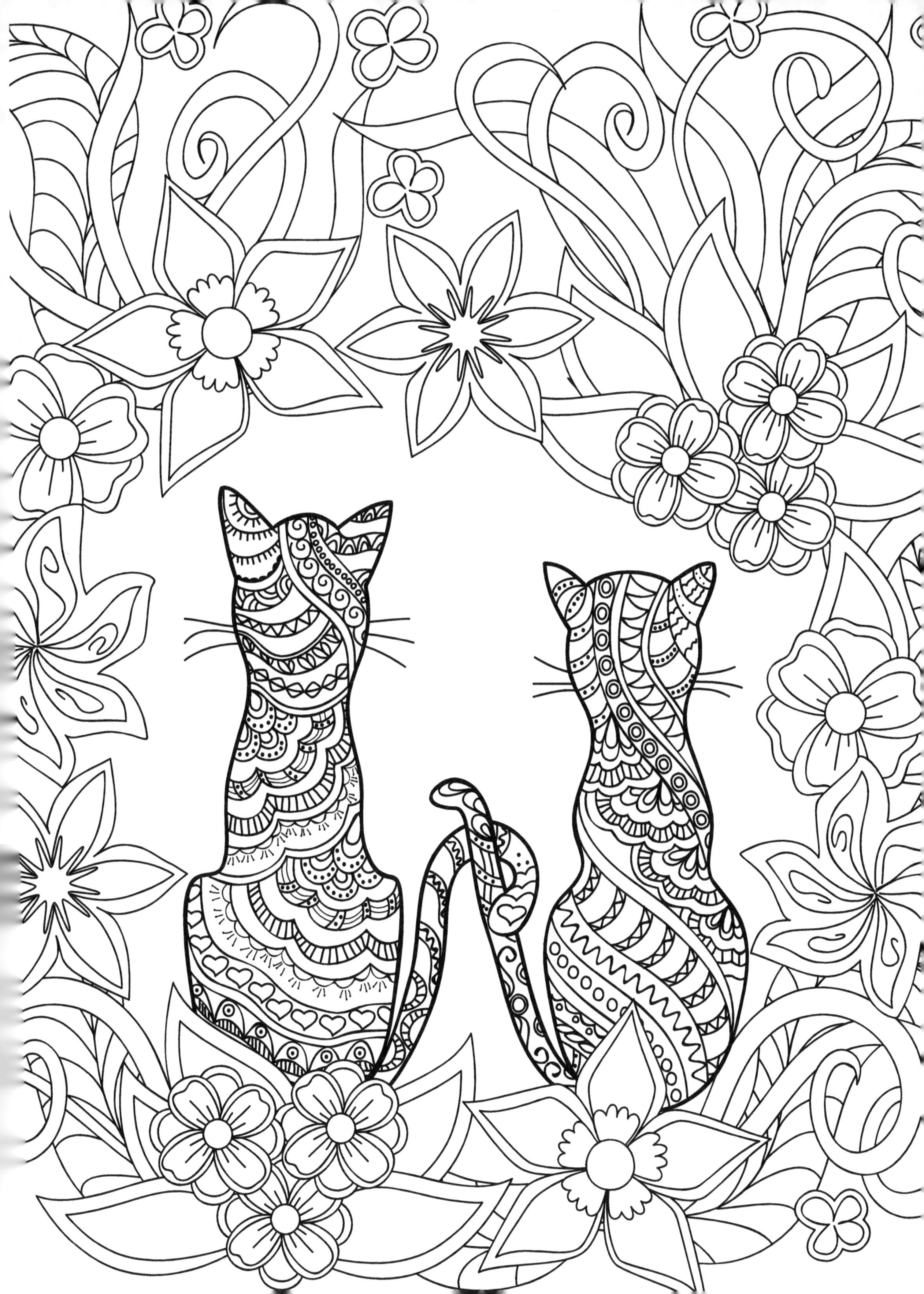

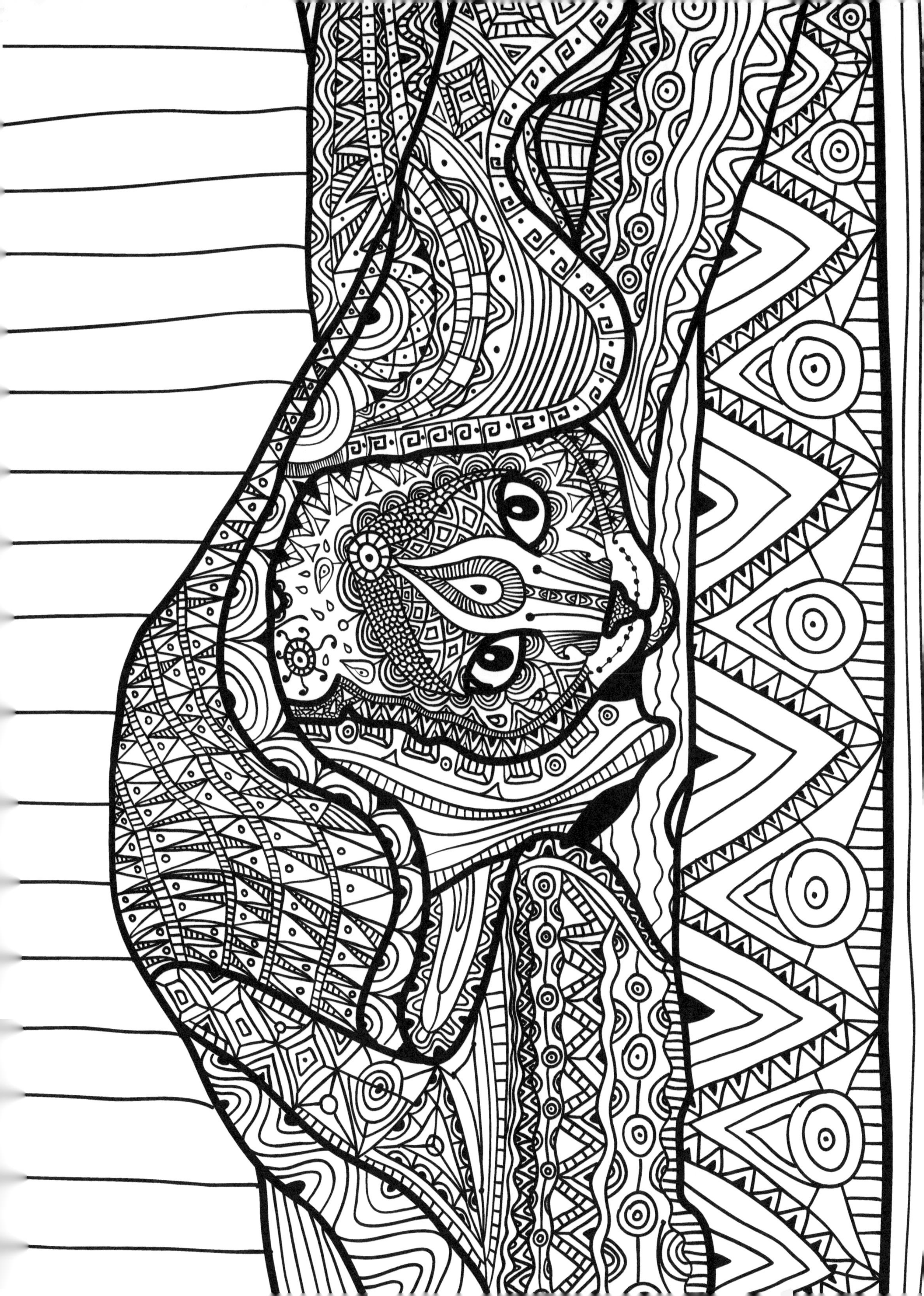

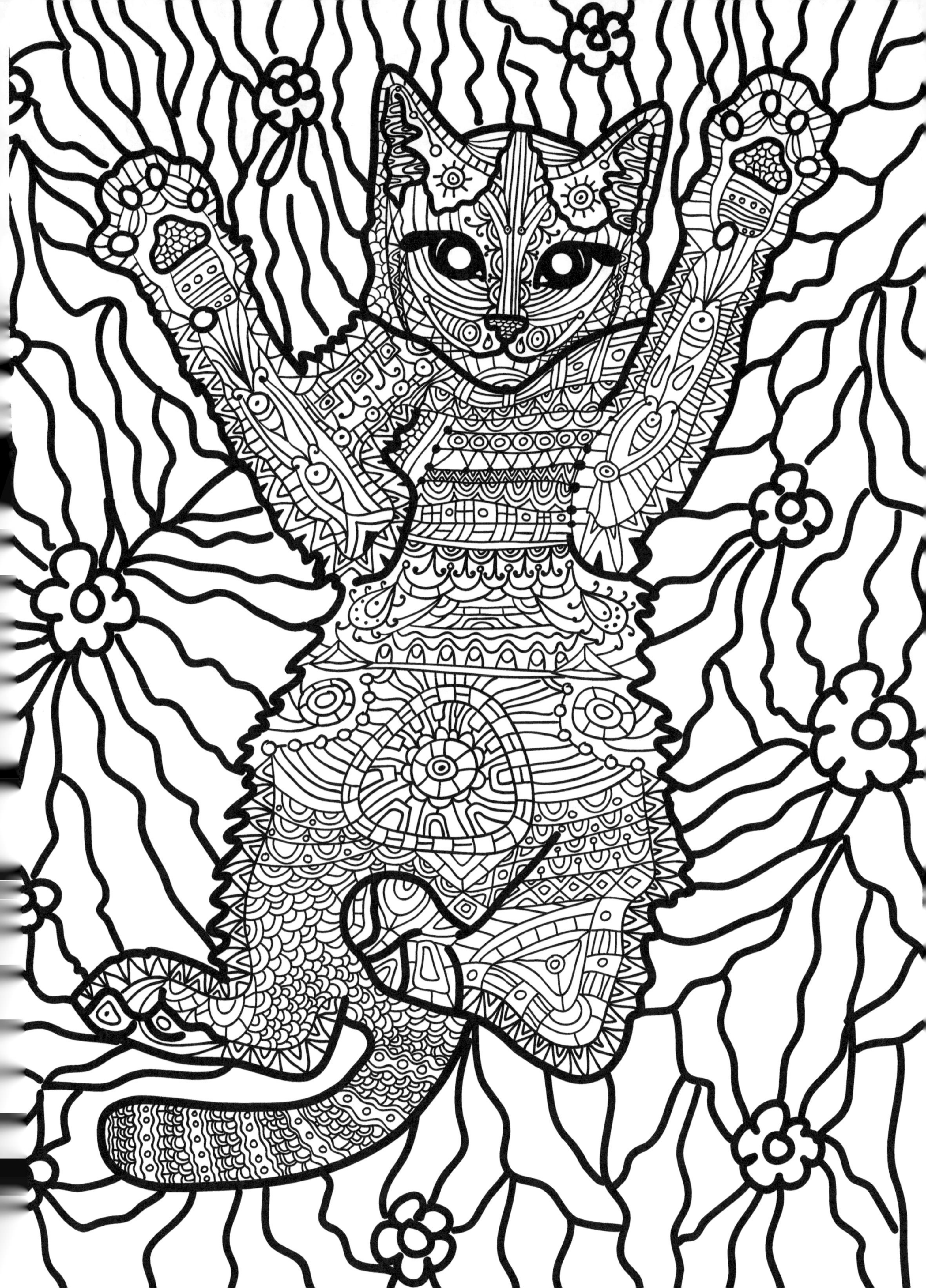

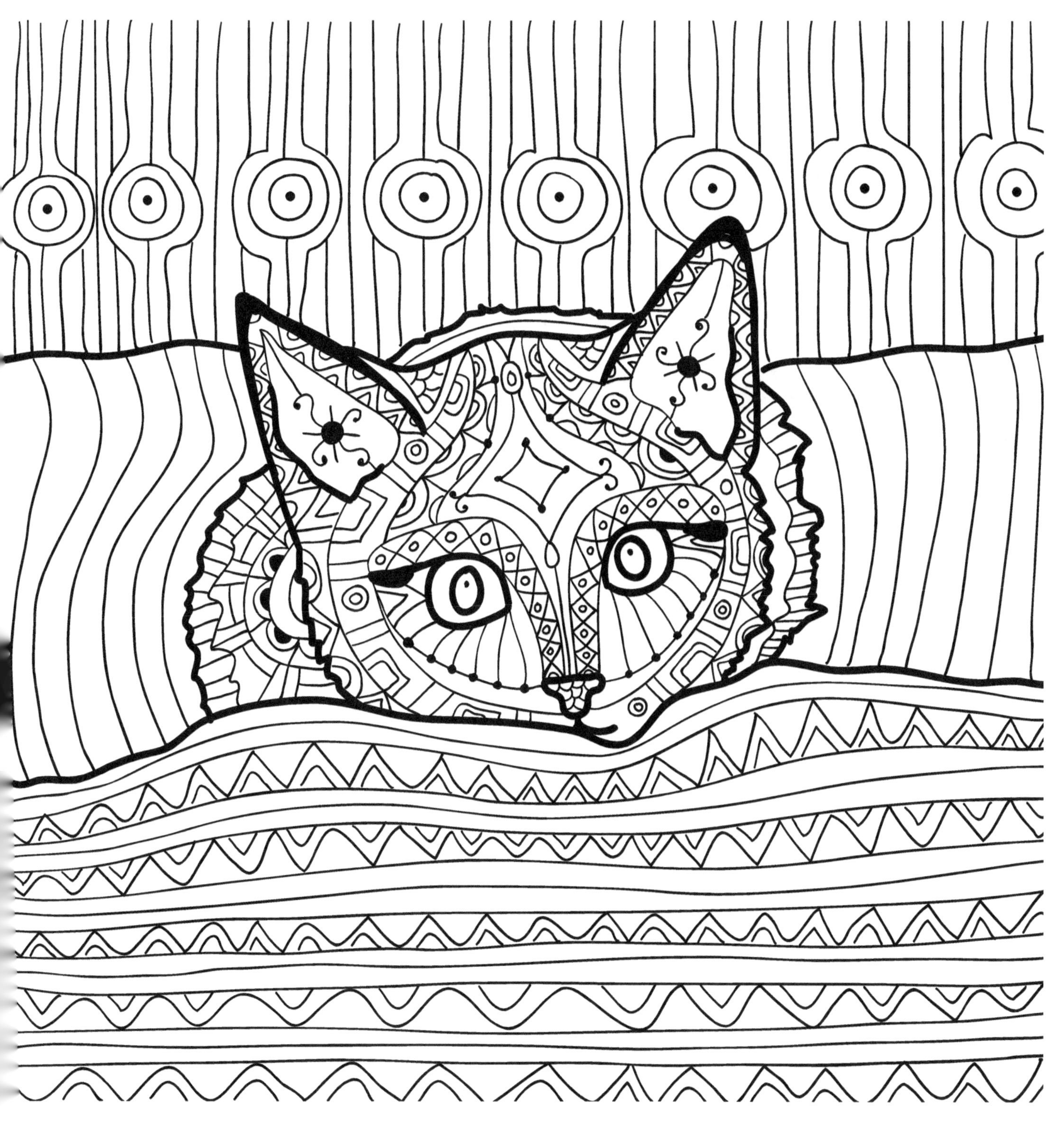

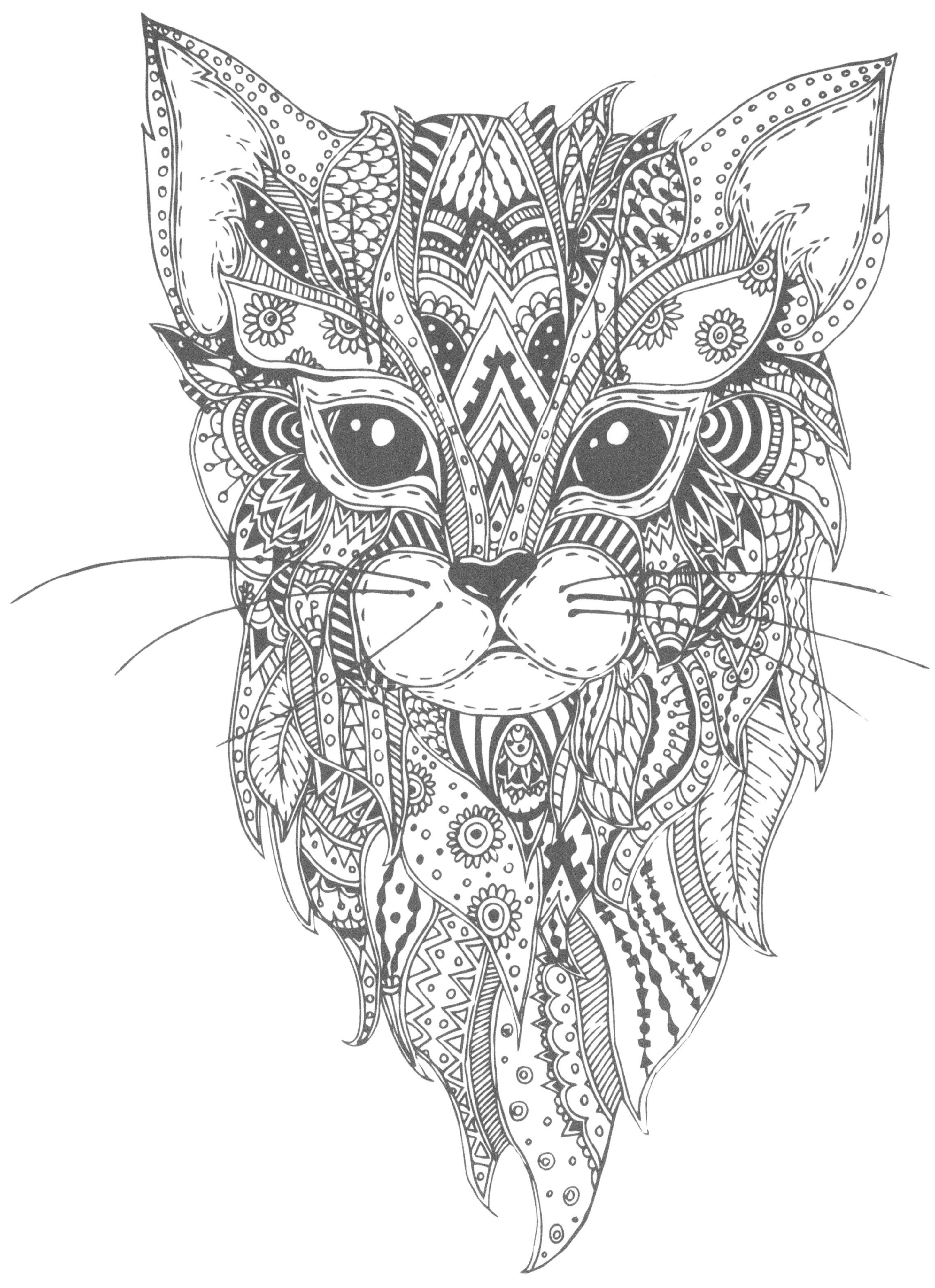

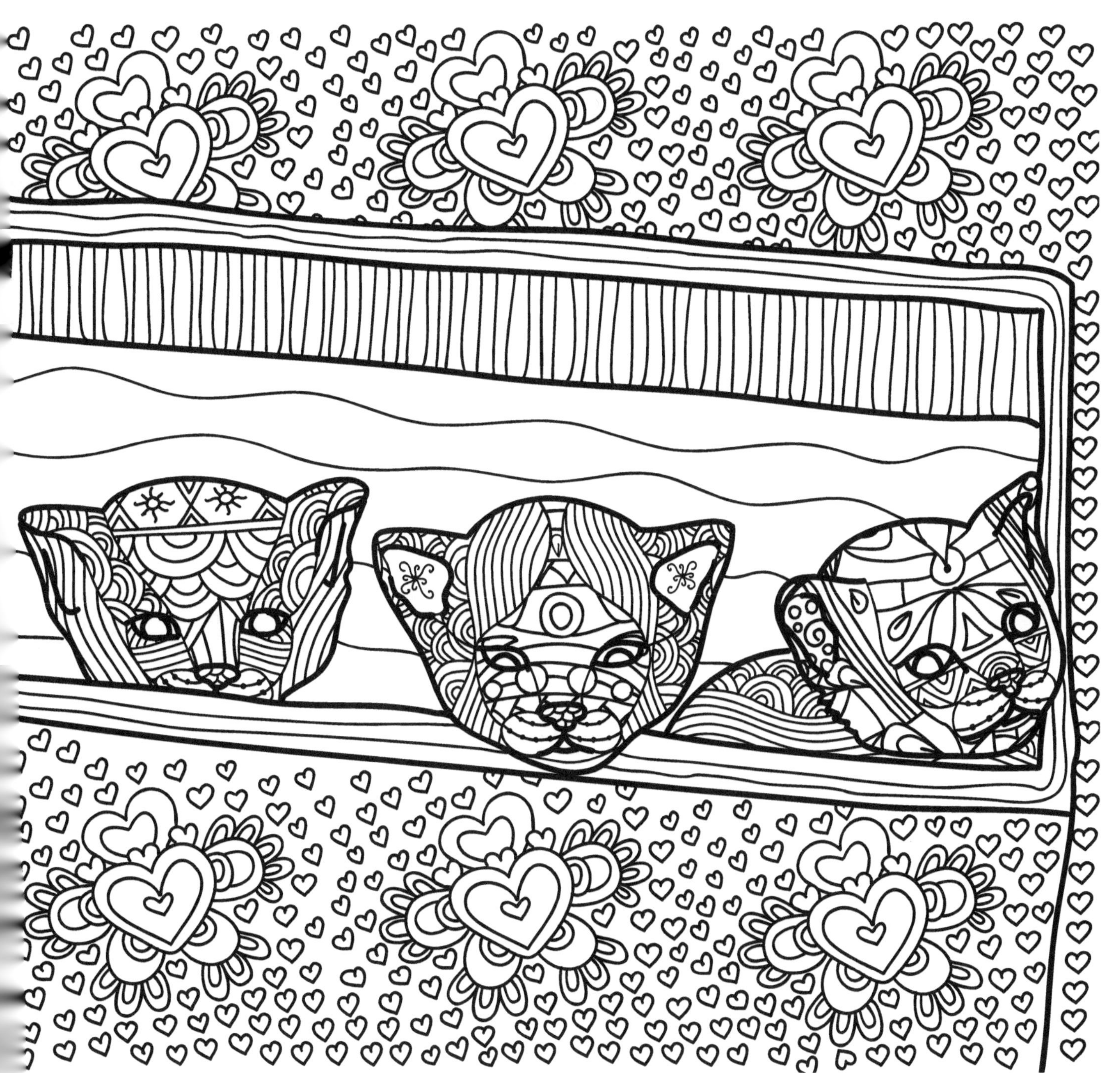

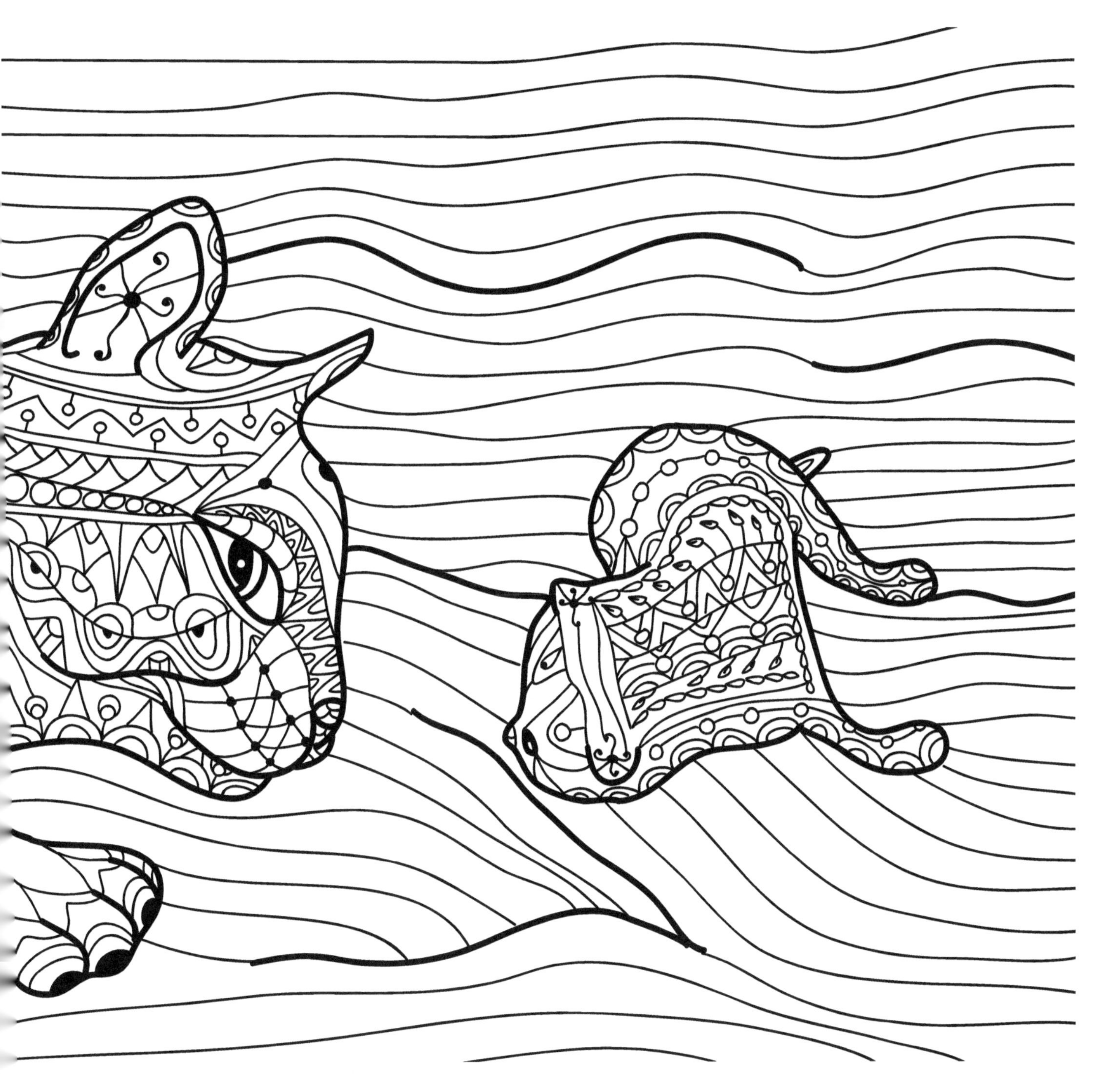

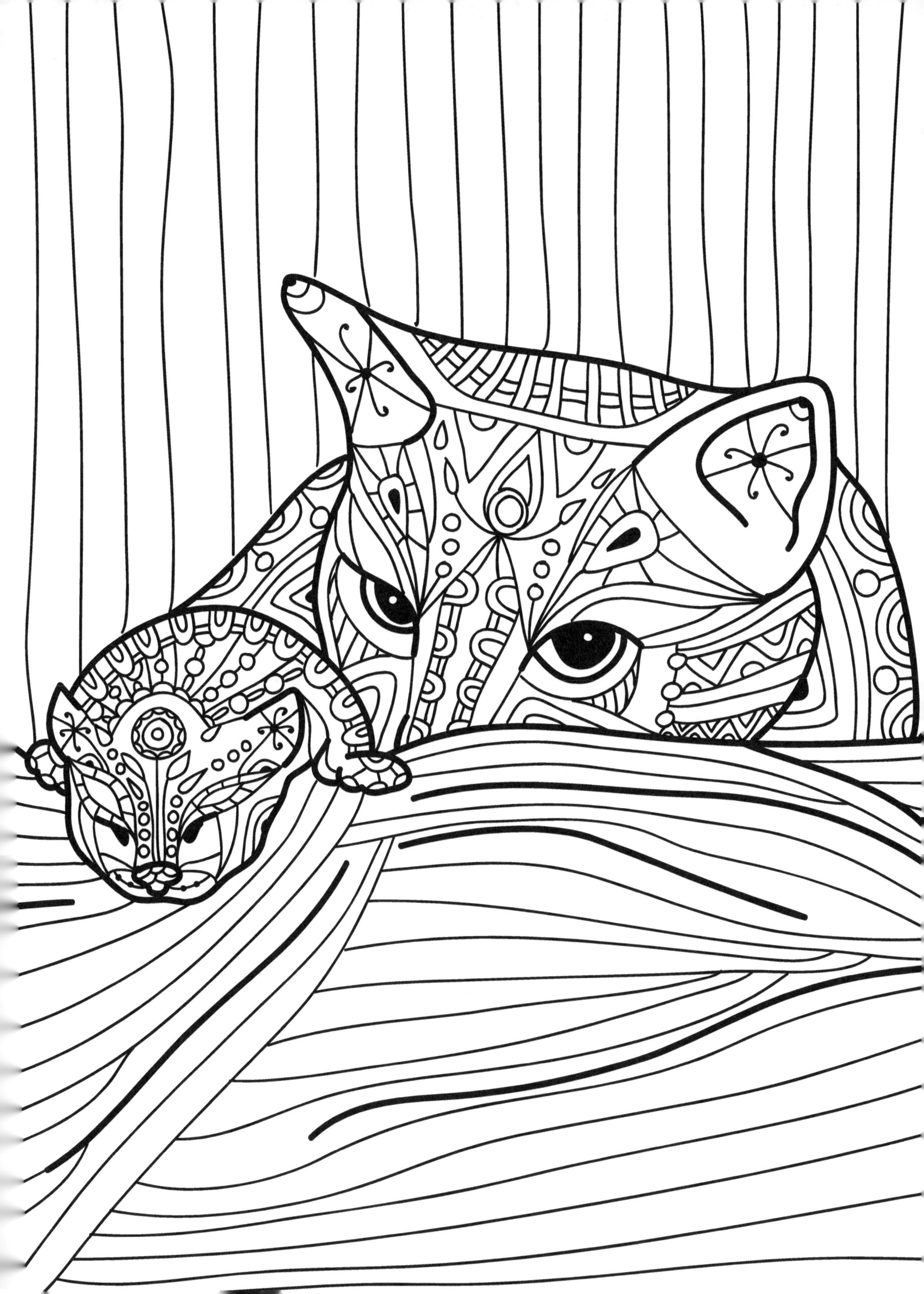

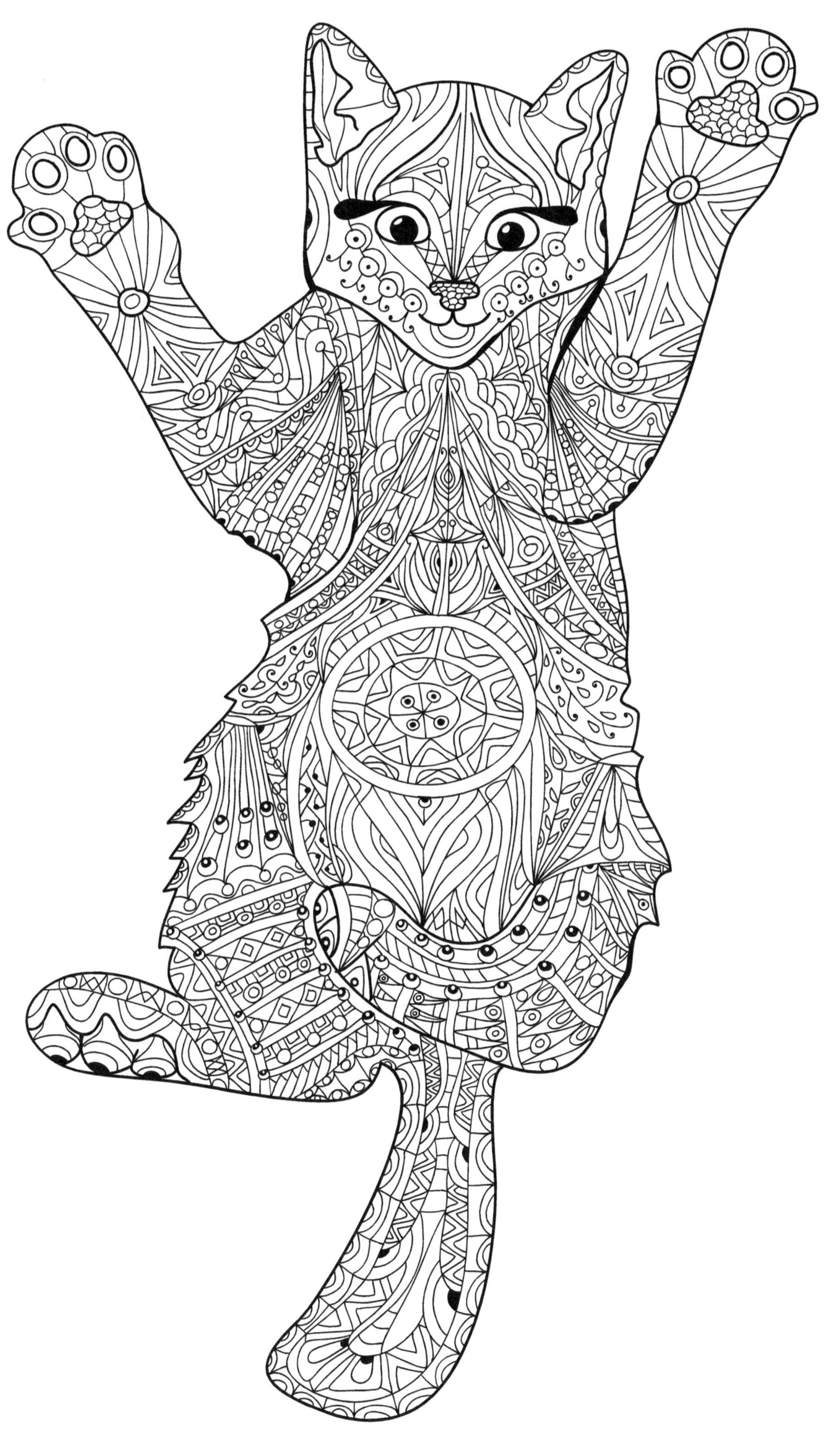

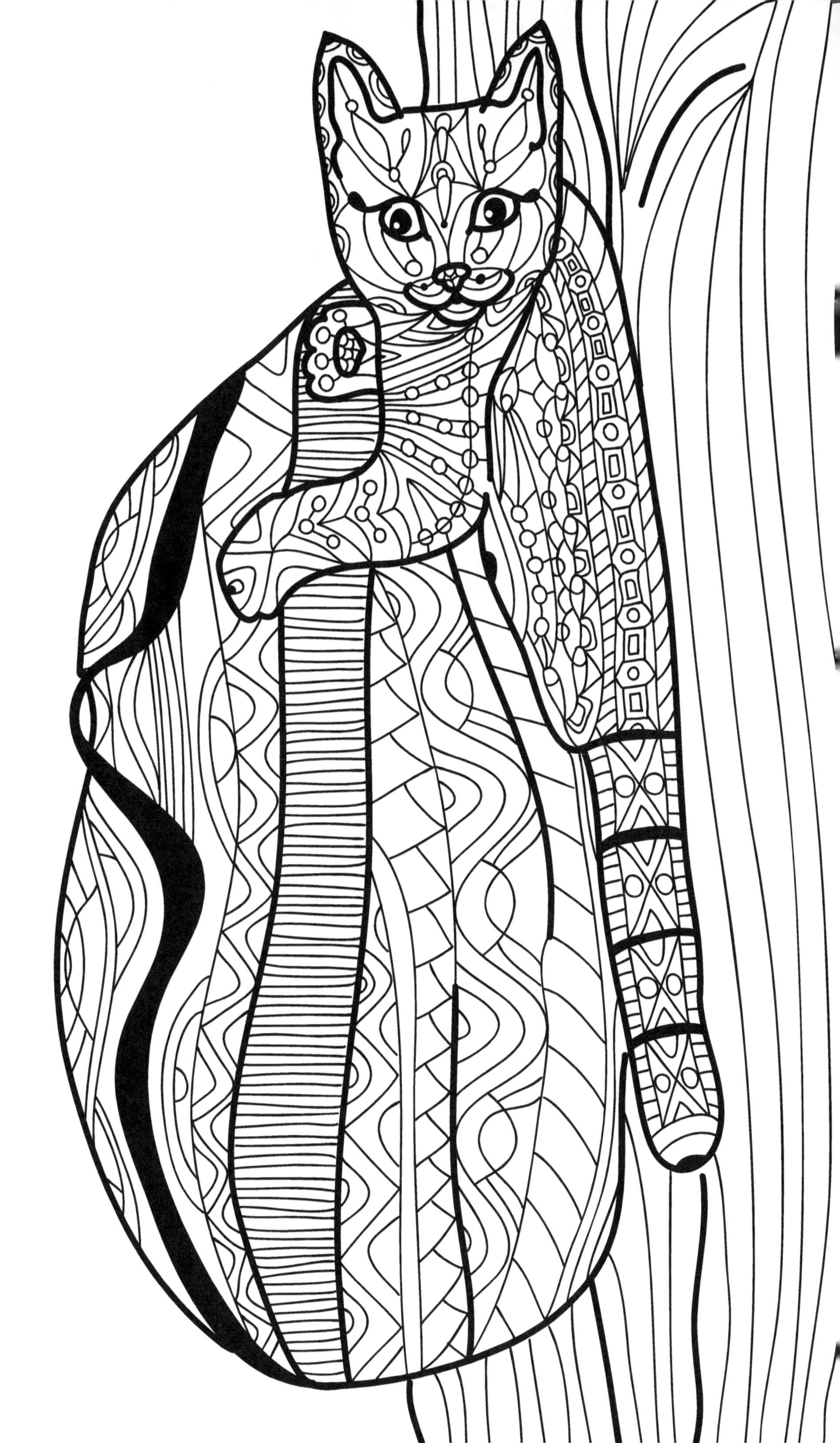

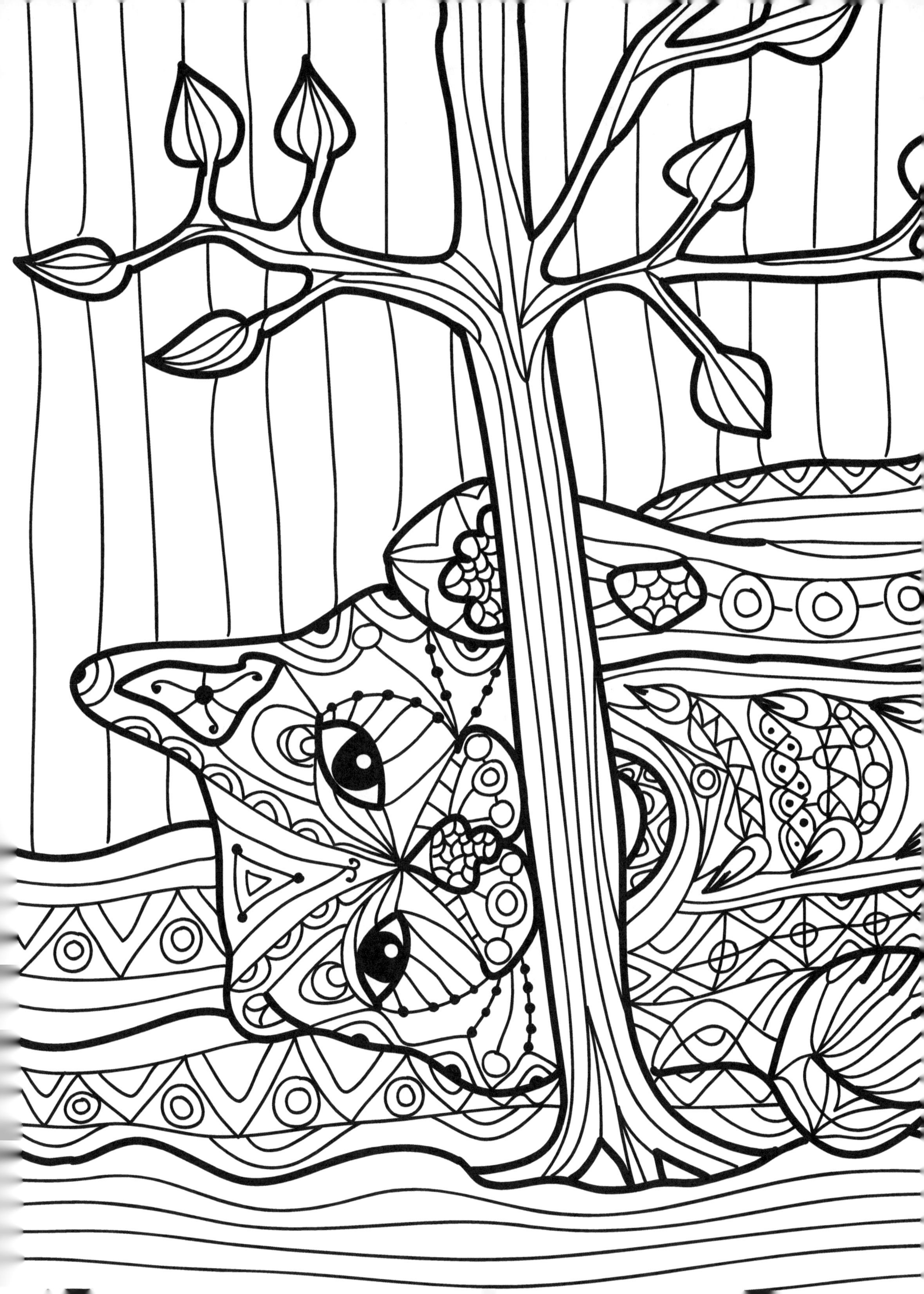

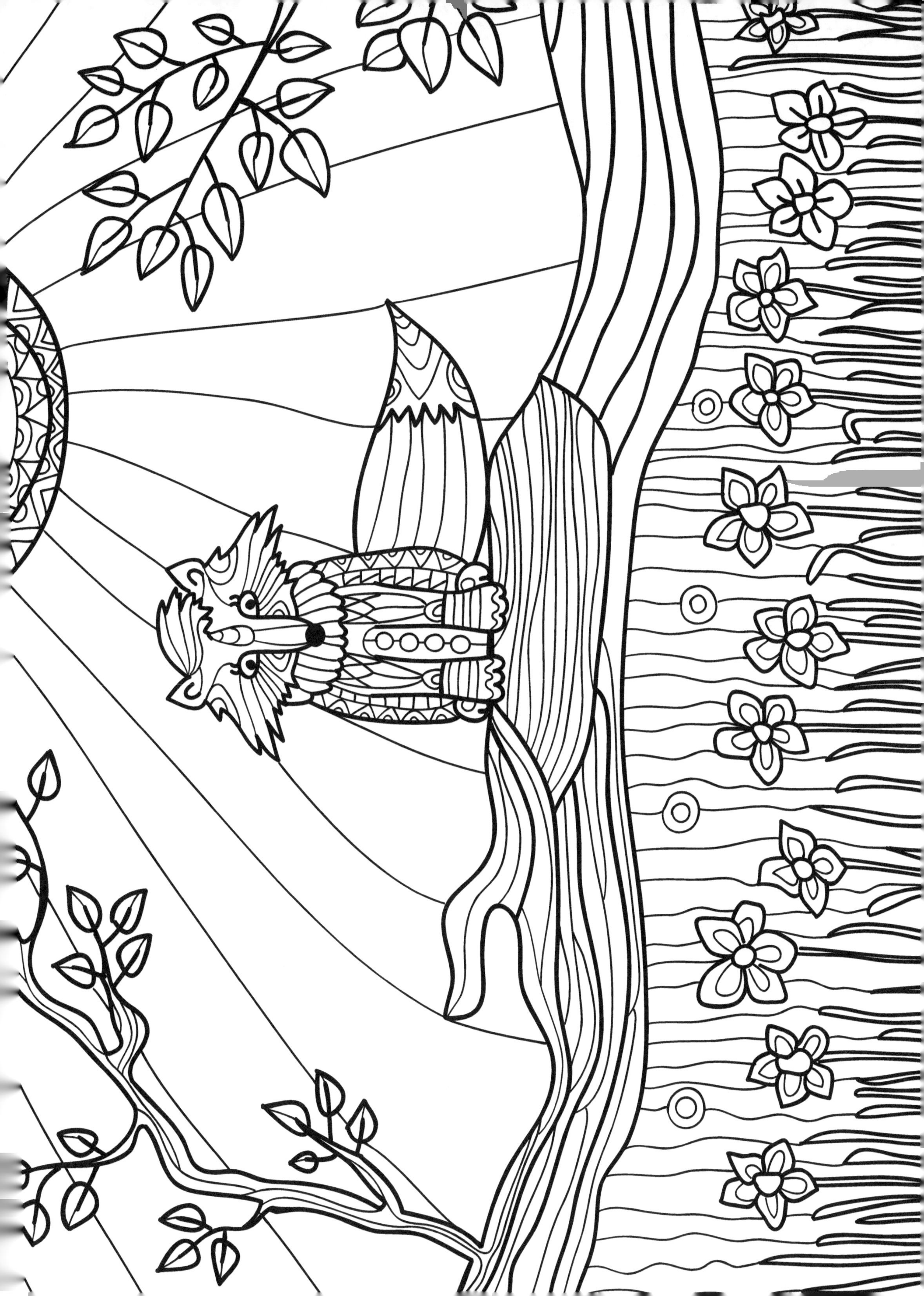

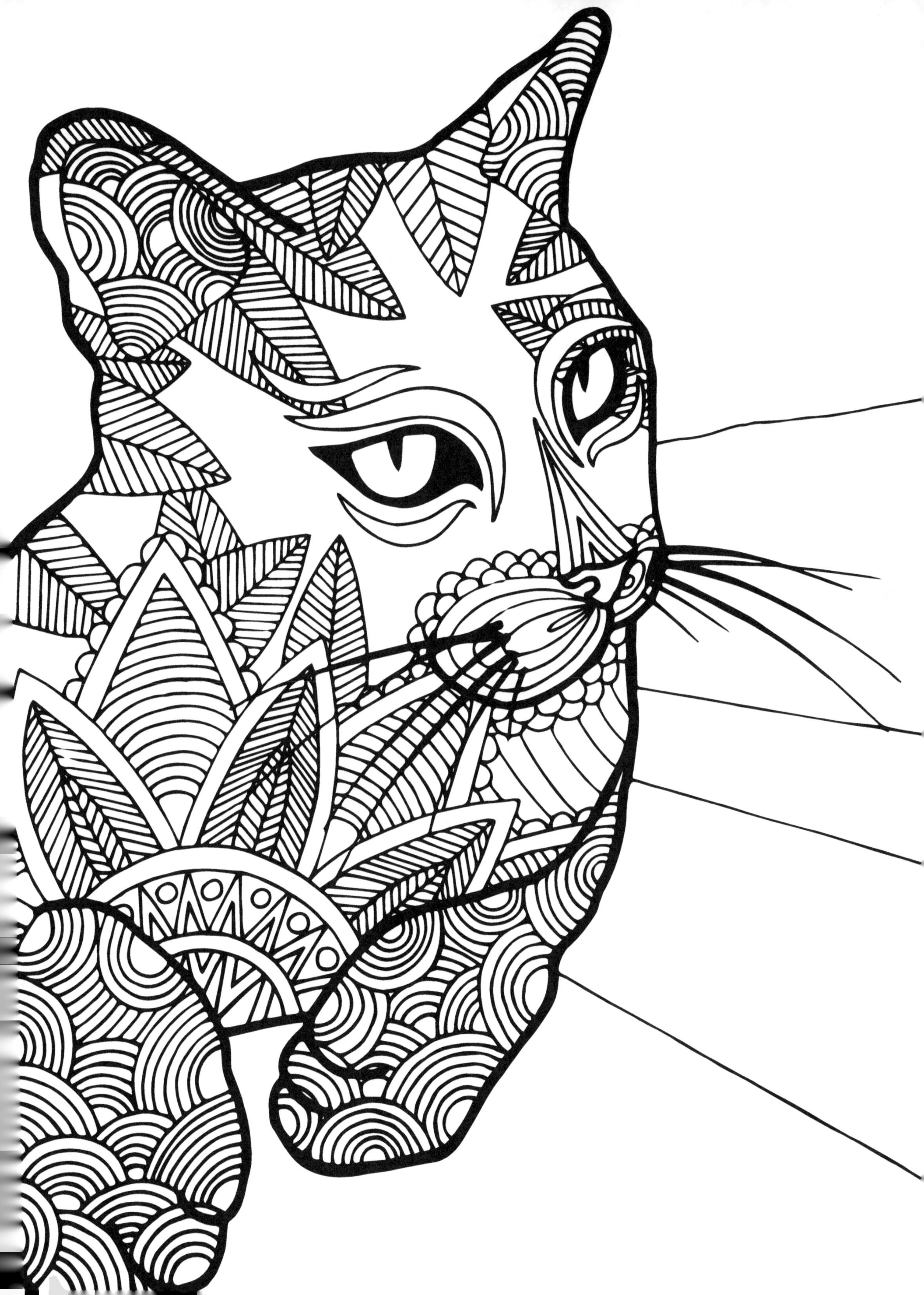

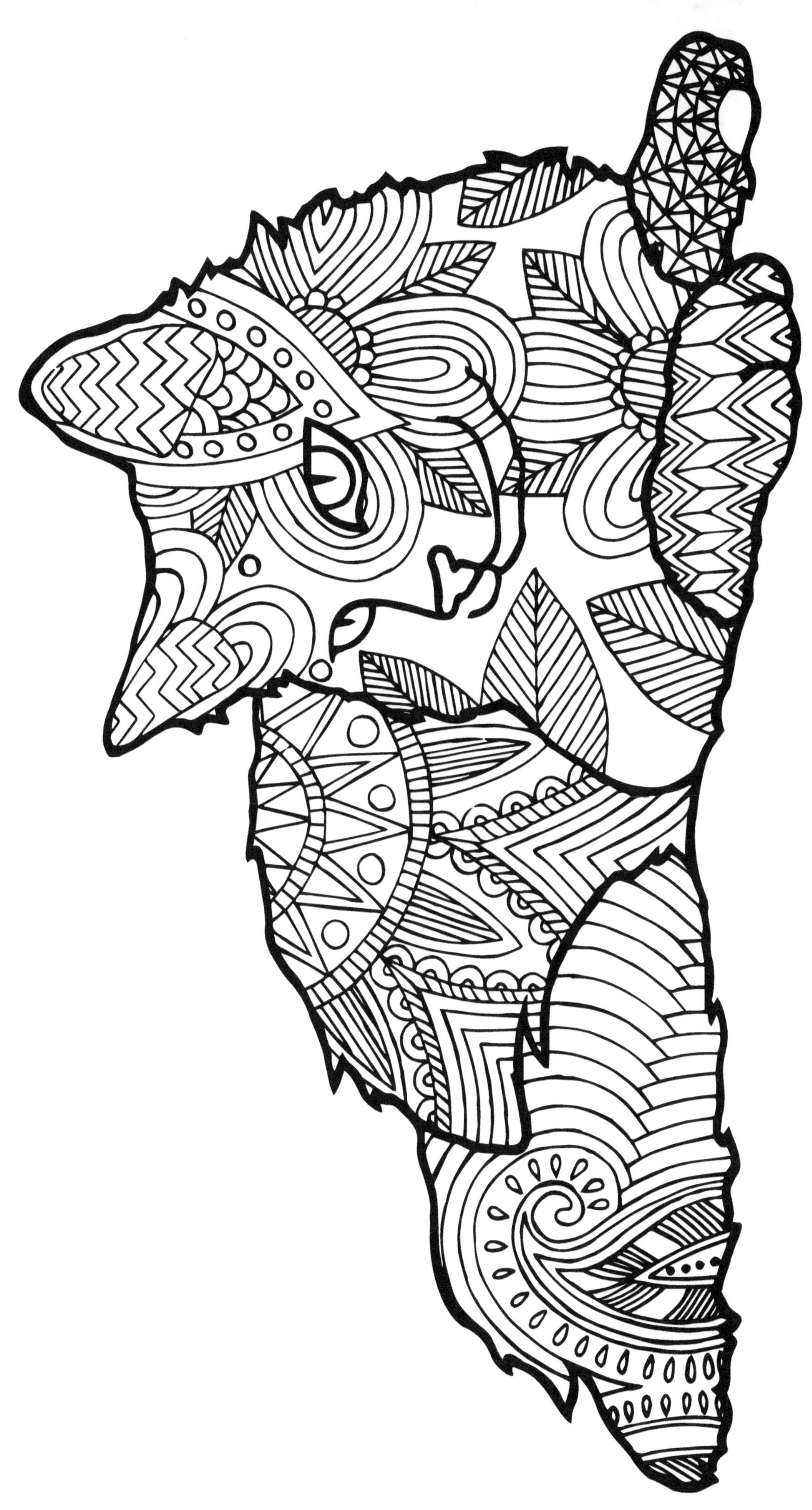

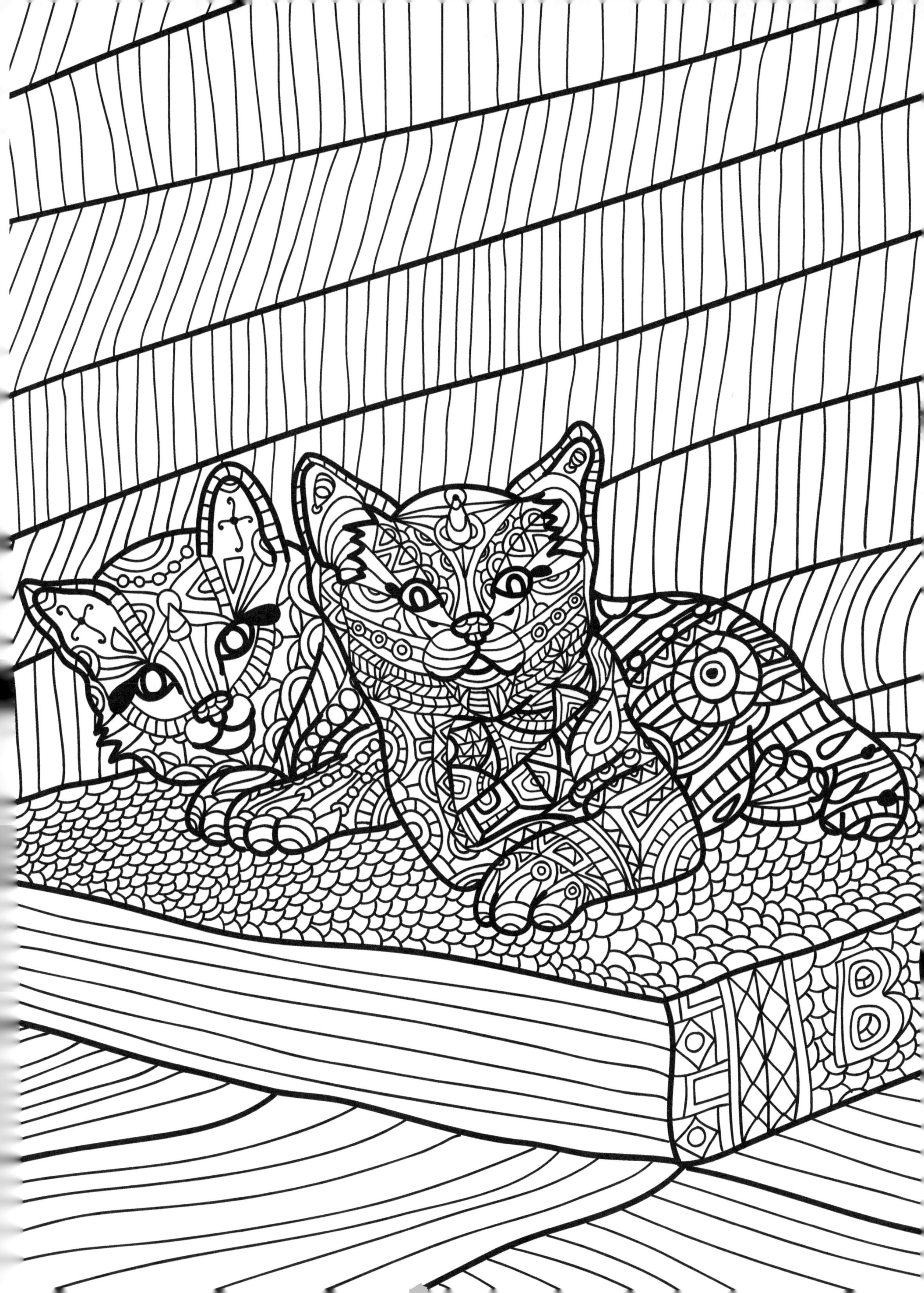
B

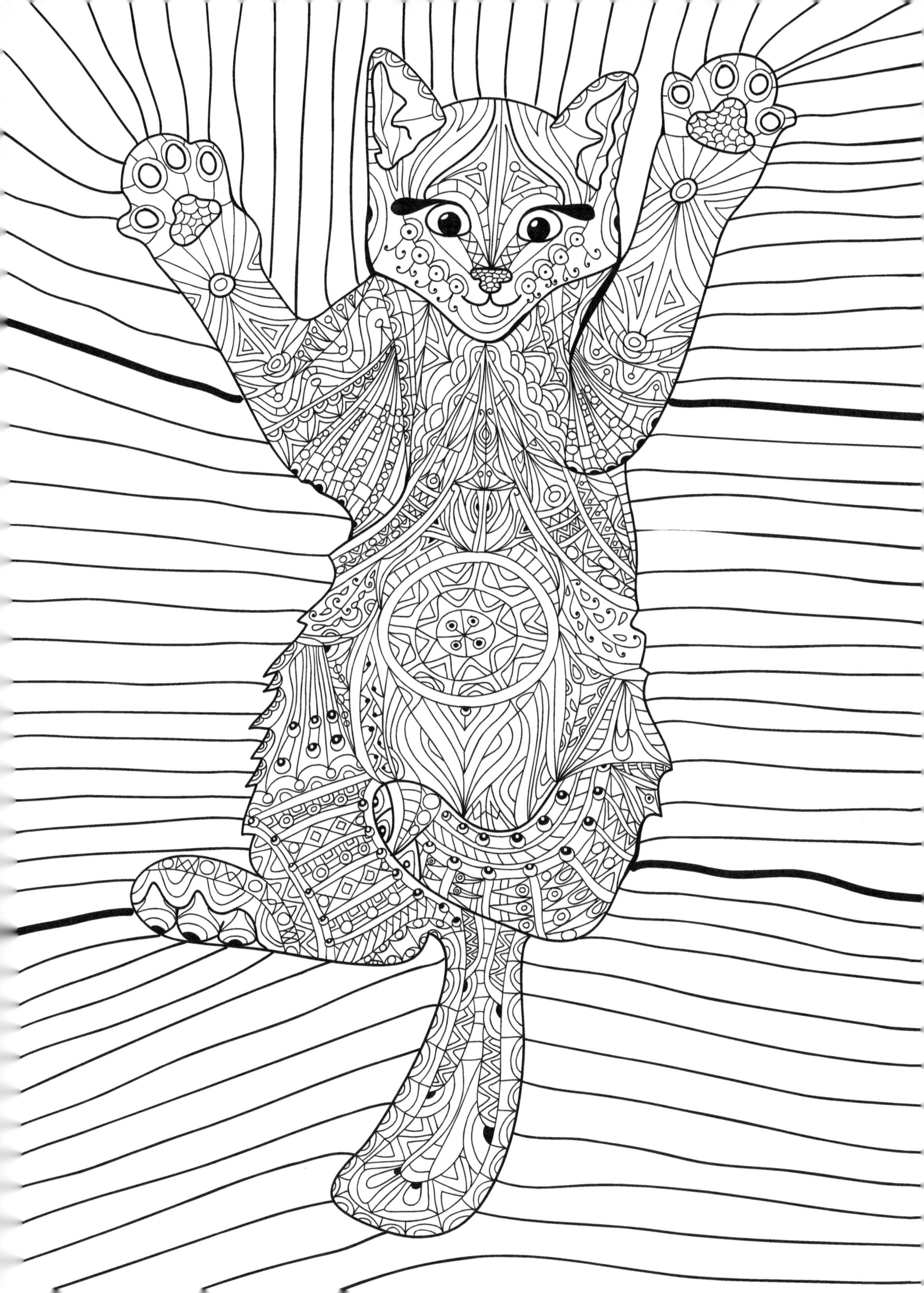

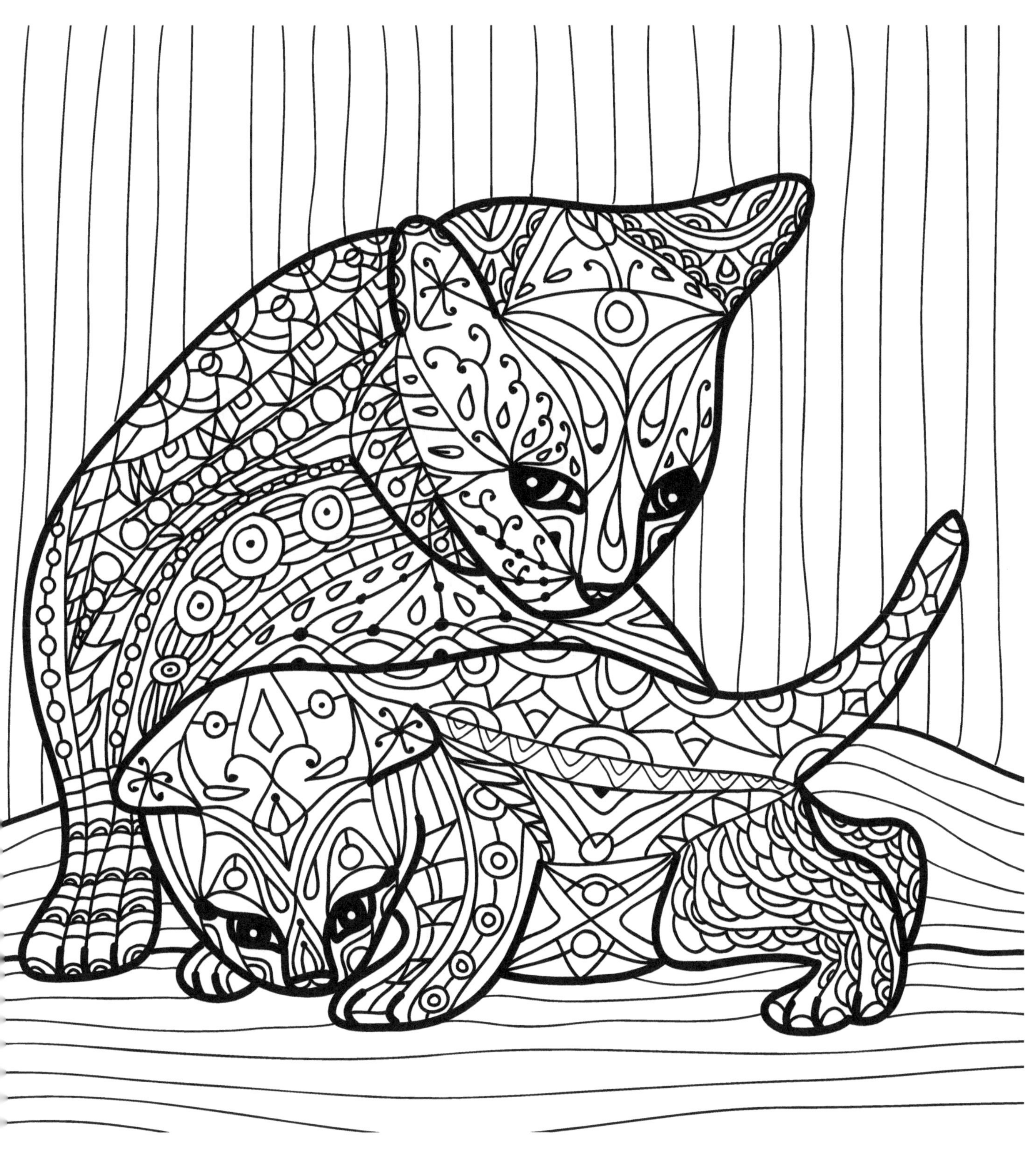

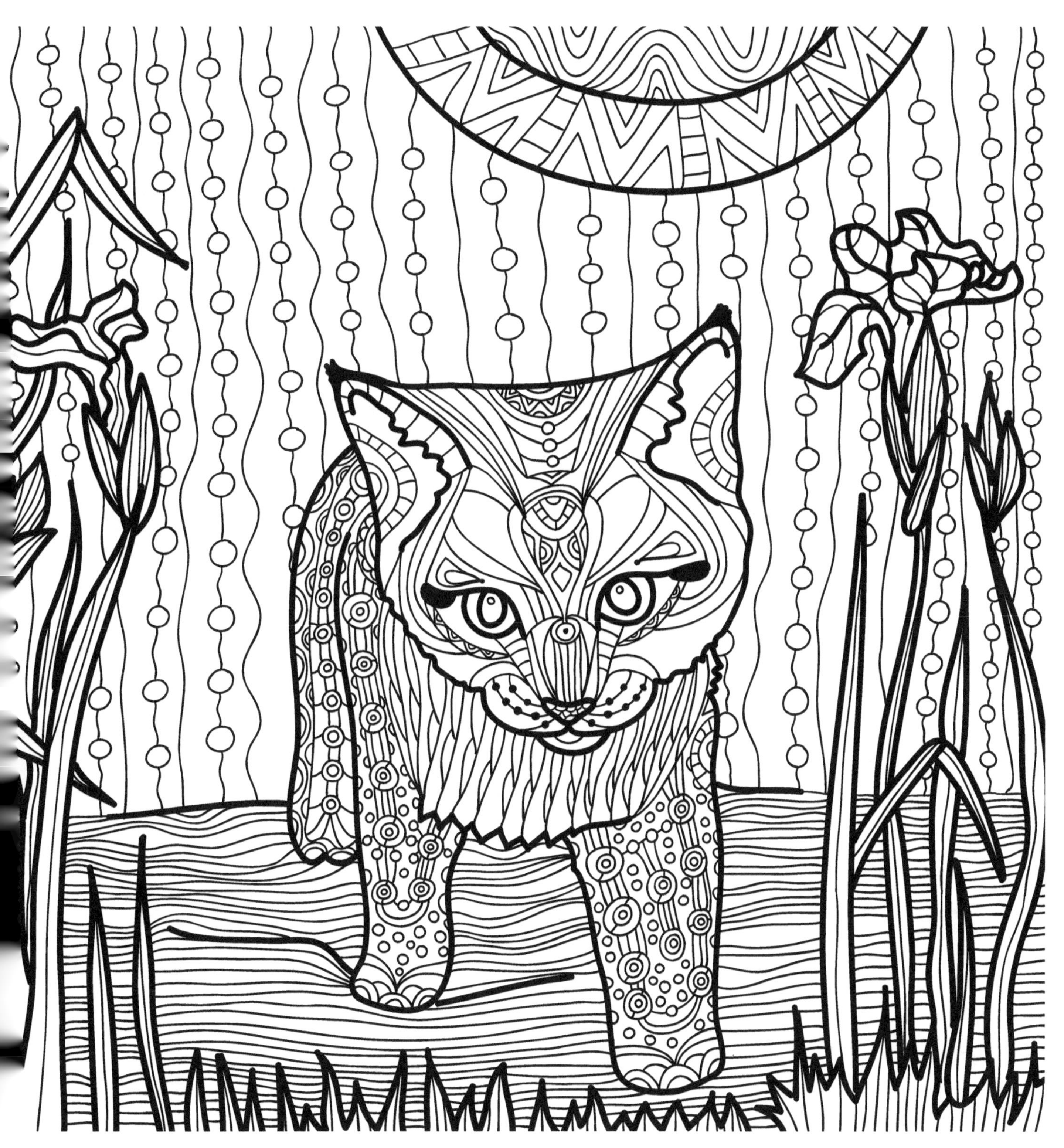

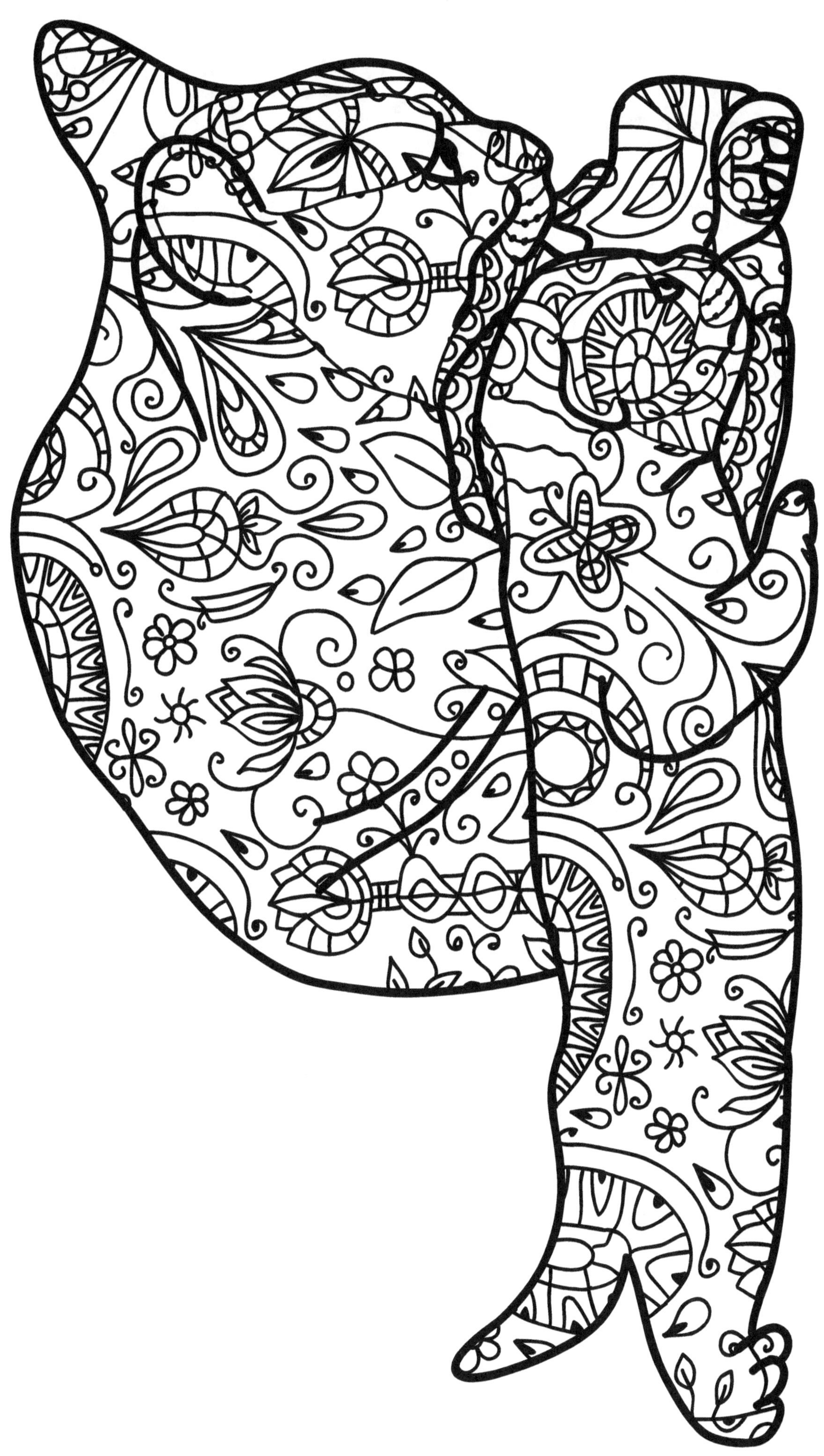

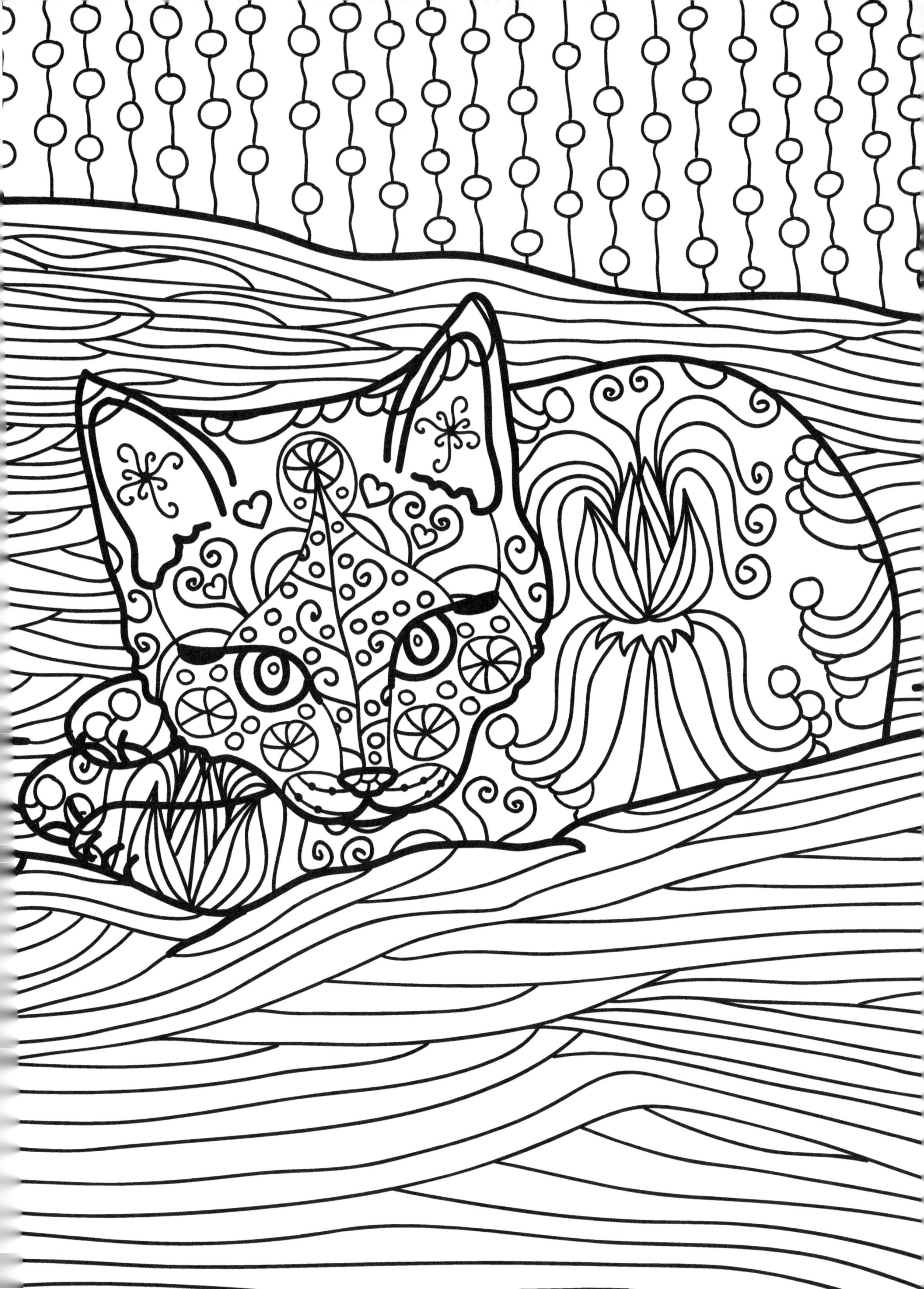

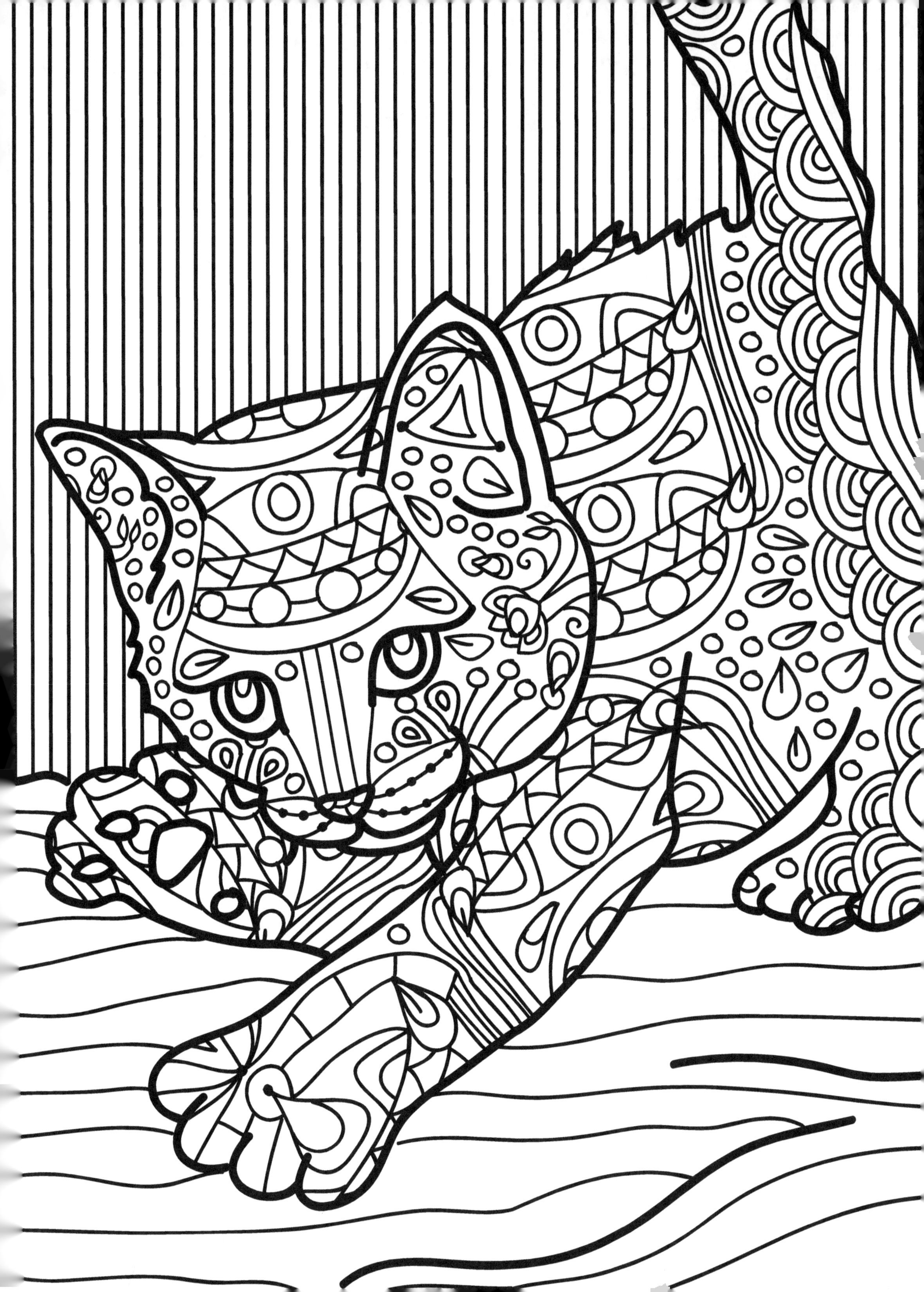

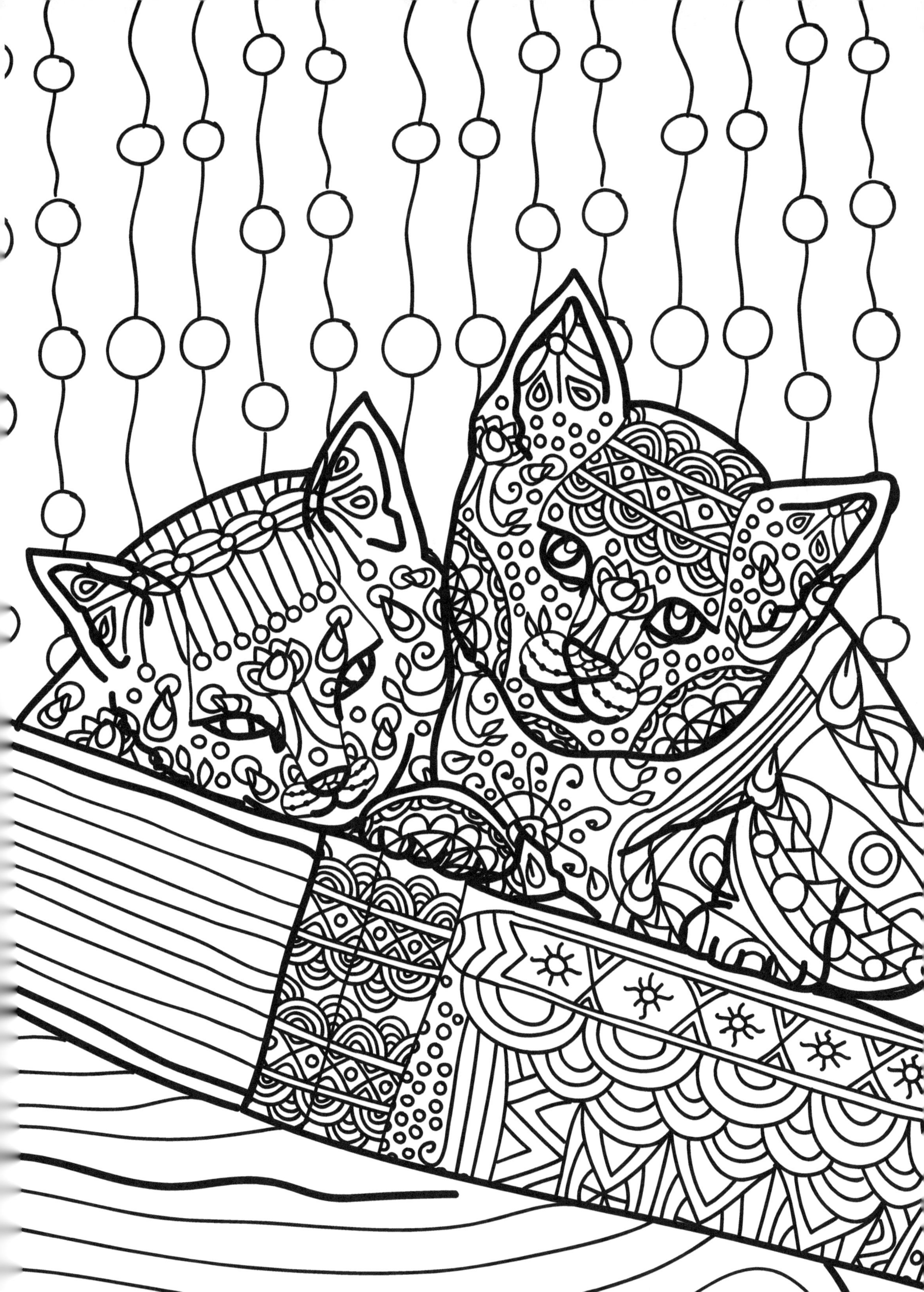

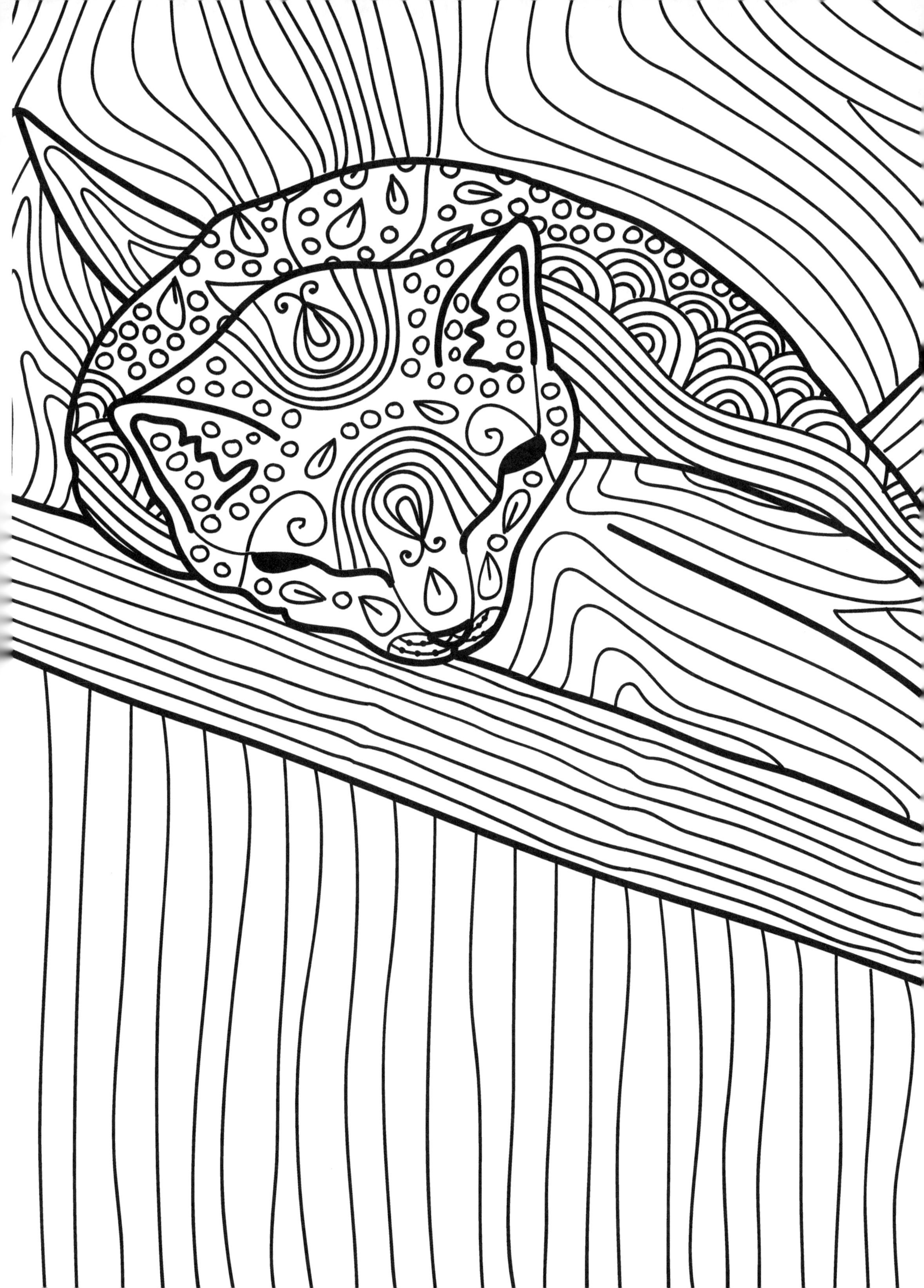

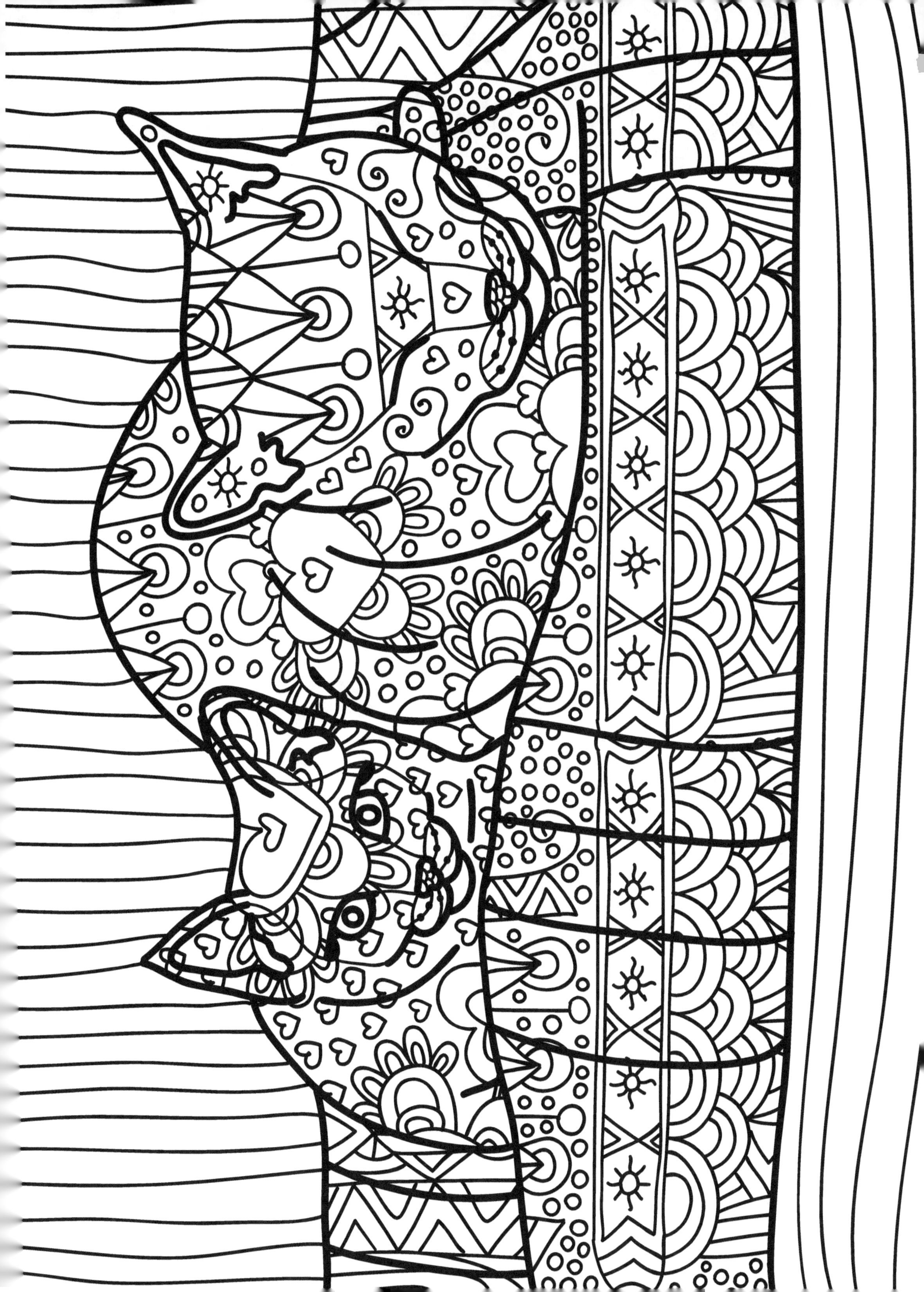

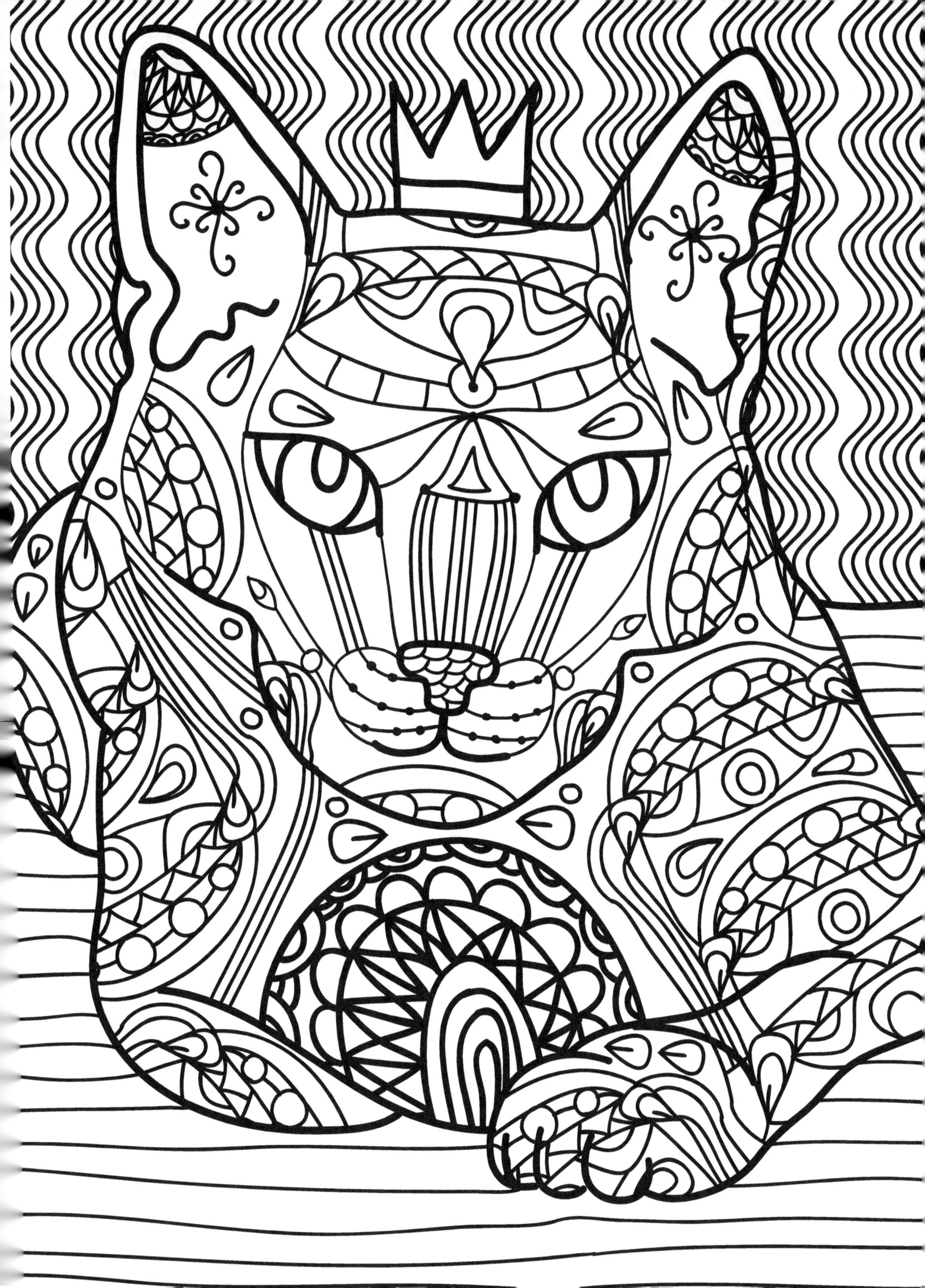

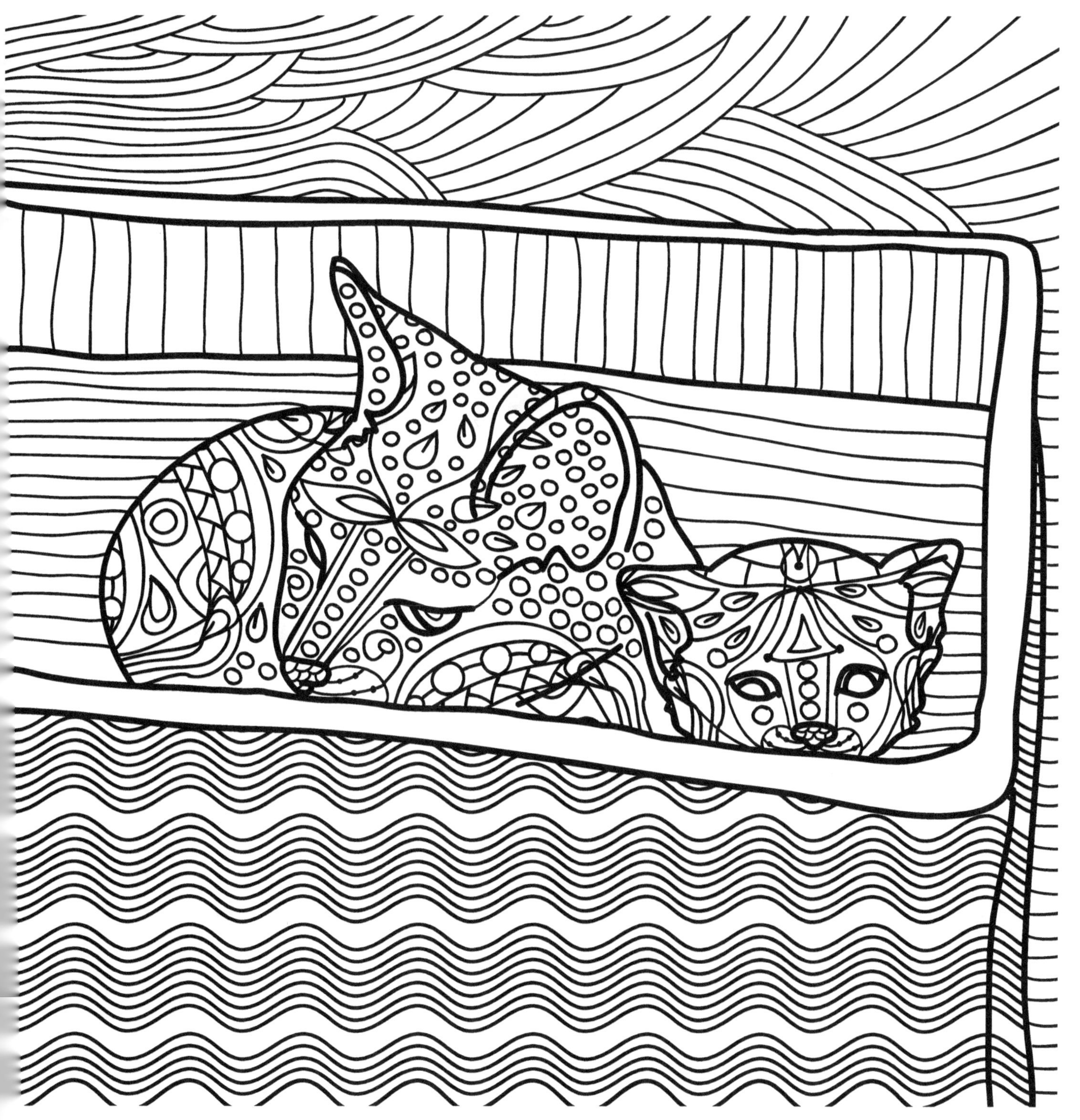

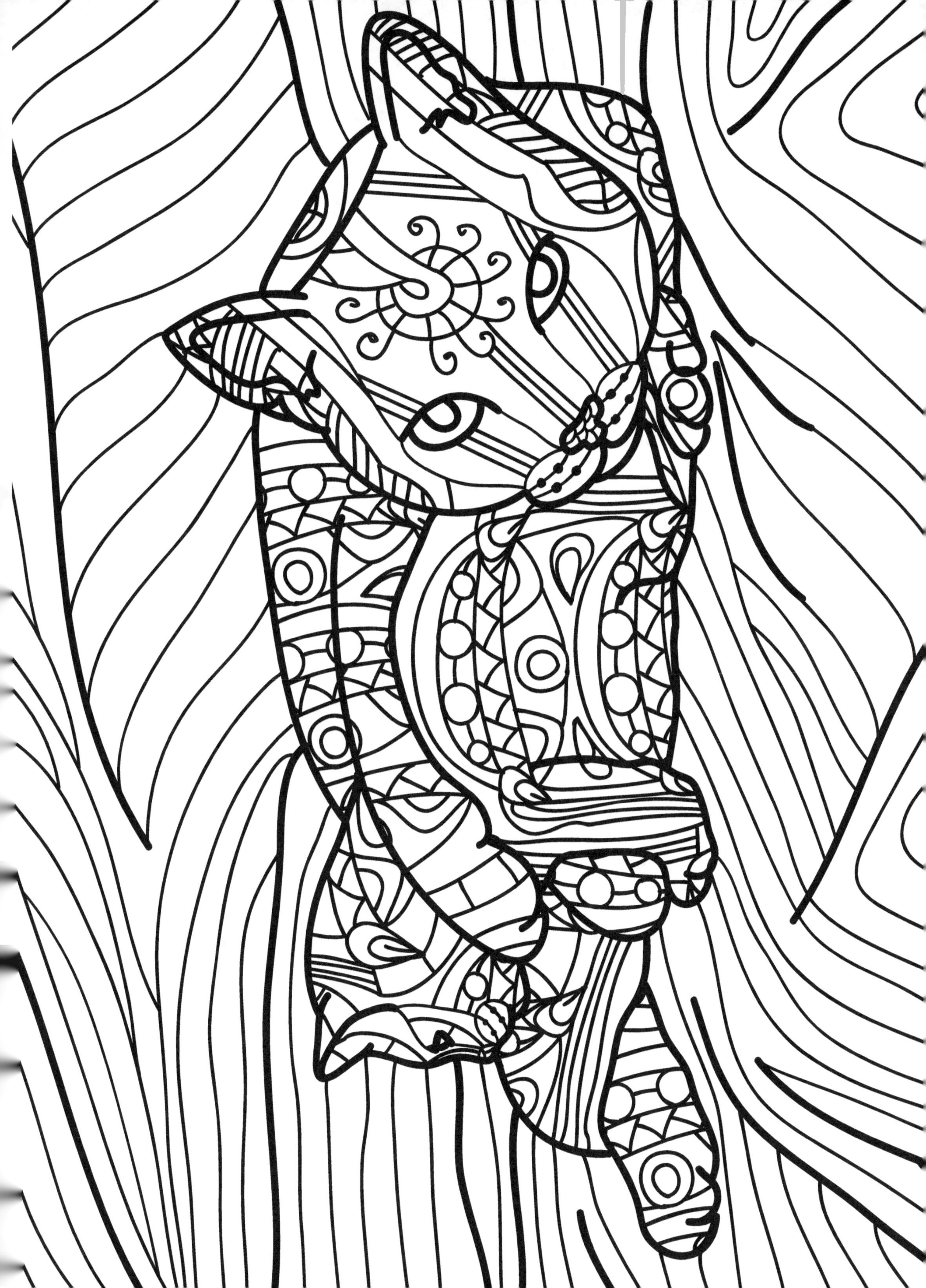

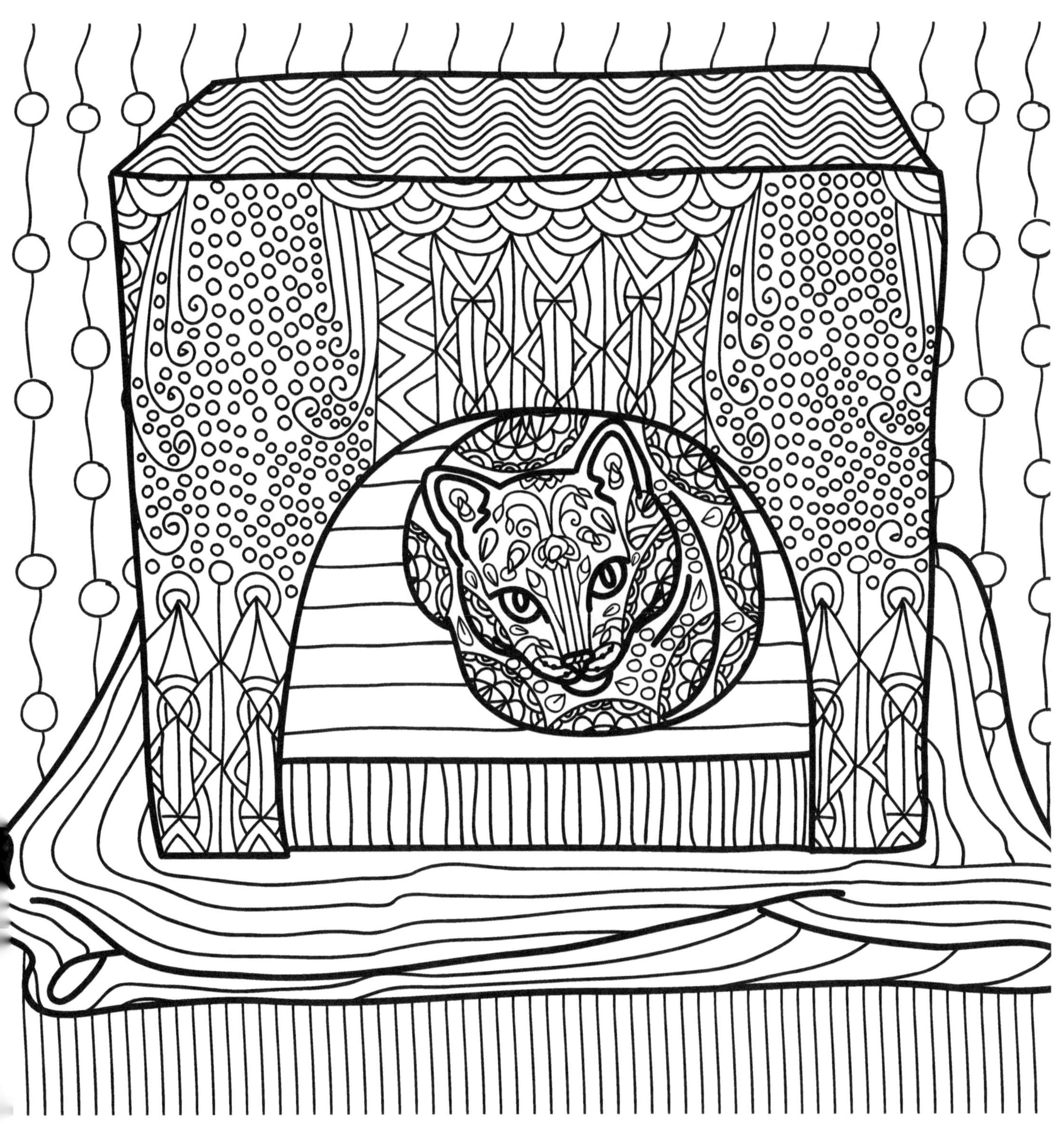

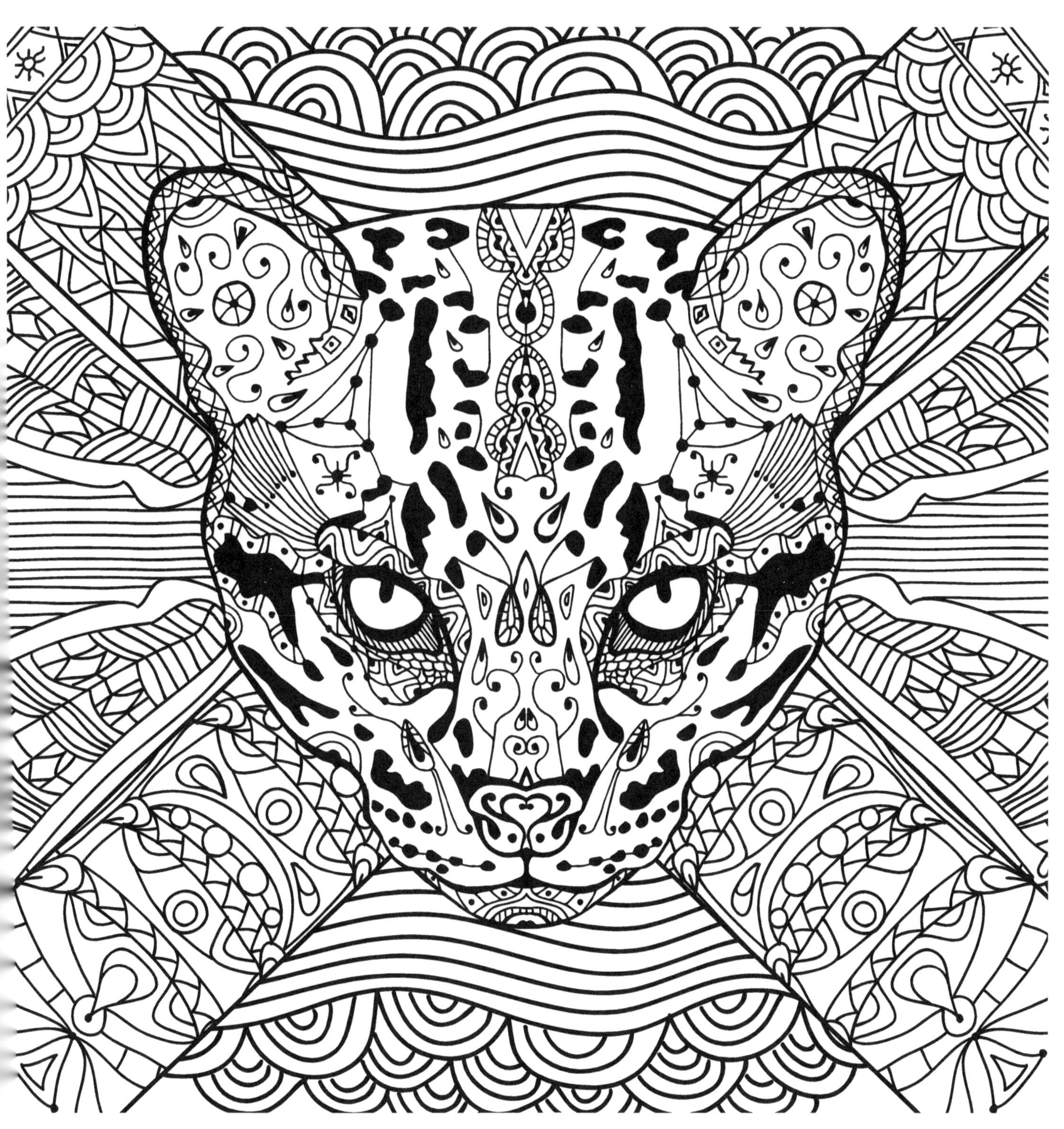

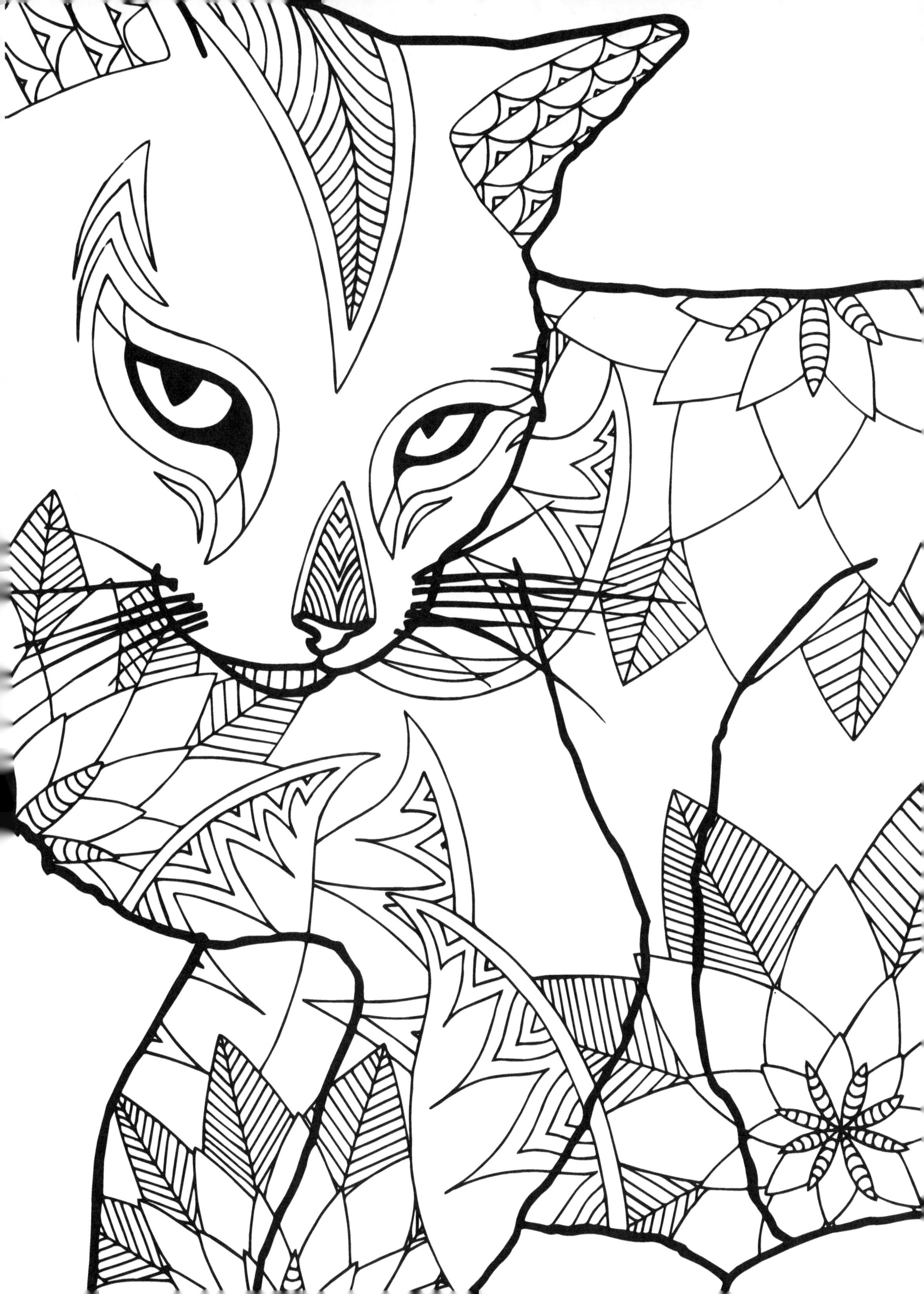

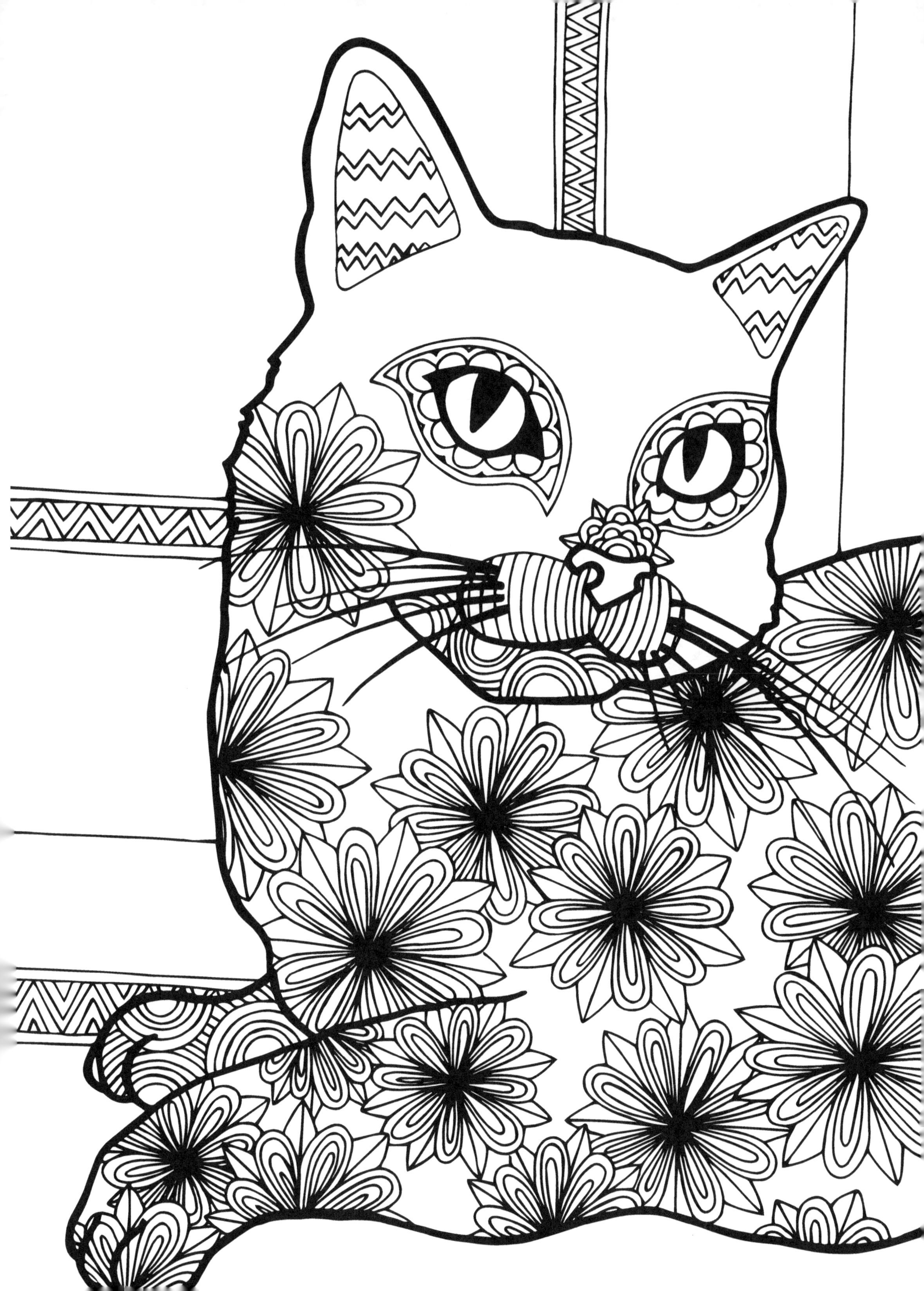

www.ingramcontent.com/pod-product-compliance
Lightning Source LLC
LaVergne TN
LVHW061256100826
845148LV00008B/1140

9781785952289